REPARATIONS 101

BRIDGING AMERICA'S RACIAL & ECONOMIC DIVIDE

K. SNYDER

POWER MEDIA GROUP INTL

Published by Power Media Group INTL

Copyright @2023 by Kenneth Snyder

All rights reserved

First published in 2023

Manufactured in the United States

ISBN 979-8-89121-842-0

Notice: The information in this book is true and complete to the best of our knowledge. It is offered without guarantee on the part of the author or Power Media Group INTL. The author and Power Media Group INTL disclaim all liability in connection with the use of this book.

All rights reserved. No part of this book may be reproduced or transmitted in any form whatsoever without prior written permission from the publisher except in the case of brief quotations embodied in critical articles and reviews.

DEDICATION

TO GAVIN NEWSOM

THE ABRAHAM LINCOLN
OF OUR TIME

TABLE OF CONTENTS

The first slave auction in New Amsterdam, today's Manhattan which took place in 1655.

DEDICATION	3
INTRODUCTION	7
CHAPTER 1	
ROOTS OF REPARATIONS: HOW WE GOT HERE	9
CHAPTER 2	
THE IMPACT: ECONOMICS IN BLACK AND WHITE	27
CHAPTER 3	
REPARATIONS: WHAT ARE THEY? WHO GETS THEM? WHO PAYS? AND WHY?	33
CHAPTER 4	
THE REMEDY: THE CASE FOR FINANCIAL COMPENSATION AS A FORM OF REPARATIONS	43
CHAPTER 5	
MYTHS, MISCONCEPTIONS AND FOX NEWS	57
CHAPTER 6	
THE RUB: MORALS, ETHICS, TOXIC WHITE GUILT AND COGNITIVE DISSONANCE IN A DIVIDED AMERICA	71
CHAPTER 7	
CONCLUSIONS	79
BIBLIOGRAPHY	84

INTRODUCTION

Thank you for choosing to explore Reparations 101 - a comprehensive and informative look at the issue of reparations for African Americans in the United States. Only through sober examination and understanding of the 400 plus year history and institution of chattel slavery and its massive footprints on our economic system, society and culture holistically; we as Americans can begin to honestly discuss the deep-rooted racial inequalities that persist to this day and more importantly, begin to address them seriously. Reparations 101 is an essential resource for anyone seeking to gain a deeper understanding of the legacy of the slave industrial complex in the United States and the ongoing struggle for economic racial justice. The history of chattel slavery and its toxic impact on all Americans has been a defining feature of American society, shaping not only the economic and political landscape but also the cultural and psychological contours of the nation.

Through careful and detailed research and analysis, this guide delves into the more complex and often-overlooked aspects of the slave industry and its aftermath, including the role of the banking and insurance institutions, governments, laissez-faire capitalism, the founding fathers, higher education and others in perpetuating systematic and systemic brutality, exploitation and inequality against an innocent people on a transoceanic scale for over four centuries. By exploring the various arguments for and against, Reparations 101 provides readers with the tools to engage in informed and productive conversations about this crucial issue. With an emphasis on historical context, legal analysis, and economic data, Reparations 101 is a valuable resource for students, educators, activists, policymakers, and anyone interested in understanding and doing something about the ongoing legacy of slavery in the United States.

Reparations 101 seeks to address many of the common misconceptions and arguments against reparations, including the notion that reparations are not necessary because slavery ended long ago or that it would be too difficult to implement. By providing a clear and concise understanding of the long-lasting effects of slavery and institutional racism, we can begin to recognize the ways in which Black Americans have been systematically disadvantaged in education, housing, employment, and other areas and understand why the need is so urgent to deal with or repair these damages and face the challenges of progress today and not tomorrow.

It is essential to understand that reparations are not simply a matter of paying individual compensations to descendants of slaves, but rather a comprehensive effort to address the chronic injustices that have persisted in American society for centuries. We must also recognize that the issue of reparations is not solely a matter of correcting the sins of the past, but also of building a more just and equitable future for all Americans and all races. It is intended that this book will greatly contribute to the collective competence on the issue, encourage more honest conversations and stimulate many meaningful debates about reparations to further the cause of racial justice in the United States and around the globe.

CHAPTER 1

ROOTS OF REPARATIONS: HOW WE GOT HERE

When the first permanent English settlement was established at Jamestown, Virginia in 1607, the groundwork for the African holocaust had already been laid. Following the lead of the Spanish, the English had already been engaged in the slave trade for over a century and had established financial and commercial agricultural and mining concerns that relied on the labor of enslaved Africans. This early financial machinery would eventually evolve into a massive industry that would span continents and fuel the global economy for centuries to come. Among the early English merchants involved in the slave trade were Sir John Hawkins and his cousin, Sir Francis Drake. In 1562, Hawkins, often credited with saying "One African is worth three Indians or two white men." Set sail from England with three ships, bound for West Africa. He captured hundreds of Africans and sold them as slaves in the Spanish colonies of the New World. Over the next few decades, Hawkins and other English merchants continued to make voyages to West Africa, capturing more and more Africans to sell into slavery.

By the time of the establishment of Jamestown, the English were deeply involved in the transatlantic slave trade. In 1619, a Dutch ship brought twenty Africans to Jamestown, marking the beginning of the slave trade in the English colonies. Over the next century, hundreds of thousands of Africans would be slaughtered, captured, kidnapped, sold, and brought to the English colonies to work as slaves on the emerging tobacco, rice, and indigo plantations. It is important to acknowledge that the development of the American economy as a whole, was deeply intertwined with the institution of slavery.

The slave trade and the labor of enslaved people were central to the growth and development of the American economy during the colonial period and beyond. Many industries, including agriculture, textile production, and shipping, relied heavily on the labor of enslaved people. Africans were seen as a valuable commodity due to their perceived physical strength and resistance to diseases such as malaria and yellow fever, which made them ideal for labor in the harsh climate of the Americas. The profits generated by these industries fueled the development and growth of our financial institutions. Of note, the combination of Barclays Bank, The Royal African Company and Lloyd's of London was highly profitable. Barclays Bank PLC was established in 1690 in London and played a significant role in financing the transatlantic slave trade investing in slaves as both cargo and property. The Royal African Company had a monopoly on the British slave trade, and during its existence, it transported almost a million kidnapped Africans to the British colonies in North America and the Caribbean.

This commerce generated significant profits for the company's shareholders and contributed to the growth of the British economy. Lloyd's of London, as a major insurer of slave ships and cargo, also profited greatly from the acquisition, transportation, distribution, exchange and liquidation of human beings. As it was a wildly lucrative business, the high demand for this insurance coverage made Lloyd's a household name in insurance from that day on. According to some estimates, a single slave cargo of 300 to 350 slaves could generate a profit of around £10,000 to £12,000 in the 18th century, which is equivalent to several million dollars in today's currency. This profit would be shared among investors, ship owners, captains, and other individuals involved in the operation. The institution of slavery had profound effects on the American colonies and the Caribbean, shaping their social, economic, and political development. The combination of The Royal African Company and Lloyd's of London played a critical role in this process, facilitating the transportation and exploitation of enslaved Africans over hundreds of years. These activities were clearly lucrative and the source of excess wealth as Americas oldest and most prestigious universities are founded during this time. Harvard was founded in 1636 and received financial support from slave traders and owners, including Isaac Royall Jr. who left a huge portion of his wealth to the school in 1781.

The College of William and Mary, founded in 1693, owned and rented out enslaved people throughout the 18th and early 19th centuries, and its endowment was partially funded by profits from the slave trade.

Money and financial enterprise were clearly the root cause of the African holocaust, and the early English merchants and businessmen who established the slave trade and profited from it were driven by the pursuit of wealth and power. The evidence indicates that the trade in human lives was as profitable as today's petroleum industry and just as crucial to the world economy. The legacy of this pursuit of profit can still be seen and felt today both by the perpetrators and its victims.

SECTION 2: 1700-1800: AMERICAN COMMERCE, REVOLUTION AND THE BIRTH OF THE UNITED STATES.

The 18th century saw a significant growth in the slave trade and the development of the slave industrial complex. As the colonies in America grew, so did their need for a steady supply of cheap labor. This led to the establishment of a massive network of slave traders, shipbuilders, and plantation owners who profited immensely from the transatlantic slave trade. These profits were then invested in other areas of the colonial economy, including banking, finance and philanthropy in higher education.

Yale university, founded in 1701 received significant support from slave traders and owners, including Elihu Yale, who made his fortune in the East India Company's slave trade. Along with the traders themselves,

the financial and commercial industries also played a significant role in the growth of the slave industry. Banks and insurance companies, such as the Bank of America forerunner Bank of Metropolis, profited from loans and policies taken out by slave traders and plantation owners. The Royal Bank of Scotland (RBS), established in 1727, also profited from the slave trade. The bank invested in slave trading voyages, loaned money to slave traders and slave plantation owners, and accepted slaves as collateral for loans. RBS was also involved in the financing of the sugar and cotton industries that were reliant on slave labor. The shipbuilding industry in England and America also boomed as more and more ships were built to transport an ever-increasing number of slaves from Africa to America. Slave labor was essential to the success of colonial America's earliest cash crop economies, such as tobacco, rice, and indigo. These crops were grown on large plantations and required significant labor to cultivate and harvest. Enslaved Africans were the primary source of this labor, and their forced labor generated immense profits for plantation owners and merchants.

Princeton University was founded in 1746 and received support from prominent slave-owning families in New Jersey, including the Stocktons and the Witherspoons. Columbia was founded in 1754 as King's College and received support from prominent slave traders and owners, including the Beekman and de Peyster families. Brown was founded in 1764 as the College of Rhode Island and received support from wealthy merchants and slave traders, including the Brown family.

Banks and other financial institutions provided loans to plantation owners and merchants, which were often secured by the value of enslaved Africans held as collateral. In fact, many banks specialized in providing loans to slave traders and plantation owners, which were then used to purchase more enslaved Africans or to finance the construction of new plantations and other colonial infrastructure. An example of the connections between finance and slavery in early America is the Bank of New York. Founded in 1784 by Alexander Hamilton, the Bank of New York was one of the first banks in the United States and played a significant role in the country's early financial system. The bank's success was in large part due to its connections to the slave trade and the slave industrial complex. In the early 1800s, the bank financed cotton plantations in the southern states, where slave labor was used to produce cotton. The bank also financed the shipment of slaves from Africa to the Americas and the sale of slaves in the United States.

The stock and bond markets began in the American colonies in the 1700s, with the first official stock exchange established in Philadelphia in 1790. The slave industry played a prominent role in these markets, as enslaved Africans were considered a valuable form of property and were bought and sold as commodities. One example of the slave industry's influence on the early American bond and stock markets is the South Sea Company. This British company was granted a monopoly on the slave trade to Spanish America in 1713, and it issued bonds to finance its operations. These bonds were highly sought after by investors in the American colonies, as they offered high returns on investment. The demand for these bonds helped to fuel the growth of the American bond market and contributed to the development of the colonial economy.

The New York Slave Market, or Wall Street Slave Market as it was known originally was a prominent trading center for enslaved Africans in the mid-1700s. The market was located on Wall Street, which is now known as the hub of the financial district of New York City. The buying and selling of enslaved Africans at the market contributed to the development of the finance industry in New York City and helped to establish Wall Street as a center of financial power. Something obvious they did not teach us in American history class is that the very engine of American capitalism rests on the bedrock of brutal slavery. Kidnapped Africans were brought to the market from various parts of the world, including the Caribbean and Africa, and were sold to the highest bidder. Buyers included wealthy landowners, merchants, and traders, who purchased slaves to work on their plantations or as domestic servants. The market was a hub of economic activity in the city, and many merchants and traders made fortunes through the slave markets. Enslaved Africans were used as collateral for loans and were included in investment portfolios. Slave owners could mortgage their slaves to secure loans or sell them to raise capital, which allowed for the transfer of wealth between individuals and institutions in the colonies. The buying and selling of enslaved Africans created a market for slave labor, which was essential for the development of the colonial economy.

In the runup to the American Revolution the founding fathers of America, many of whom were slave owners themselves, played a crucial role in the development of the slave industry. Of the 56 signers of the Declaration of Independence, 41 owned slaves at some point in their lives. This means that a significant majority of the men who signed one of the most important documents in American history were directly involved in the slave industrial complex. Many of the signers who owned slaves were among the wealthiest and most influential men in the colonies. For example, Thomas Jefferson, who is perhaps the most well-known of the signers, owned hundreds of slaves at his Virginia plantation. Other slave-owning signers included George Washington, James Madison, Benjamin Franklin, and John Hancock. The fact that so many of the signers owned slaves reflects the pervasive influence of slavery in the early United States. The slave trade and the use of slave labor were integral to the colonial economy, and slave ownership was seen as a sign of wealth and status. Additionally, many of the signers were from southern states, where the institution of slavery was already particularly entrenched.

Foundation of American Government by John Henry Hintermeister (1925). Robert Morris signs the Constitution before George Washington.

One lesser known "father" is Robert Morris; Robert Morris was a wealthy American merchant and financier who lived during the late 1700s and early 1800s. He is known for his contributions to the American Revolution, his role as a signer of the Declaration of Independence, and his work as the superintendent of finance for the Continental Congress. Morris, often referred to as the "financier of the American Revolution," was one of the wealthiest men in the early United States and made a fortune through various business ventures, including the slave trade. Morris was a partner in several trading firms that imported and exported goods, including slaves, and he invested in plantations in the West Indies that relied heavily on slave labor. In 1781, Morris lent money to the French government to help fund the Siege of Yorktown, which was a key and final victory for the American forces. In exchange for the loan, Morris received a cargo of slaves from the French West Indies, which he sold in the United States for a substantial profit.

Despite the growing opposition to slavery in the 18th century, the slave industry nearly 200 years in existence, continued to thrive on the continent, and by the end of the century, there were over 700,000 slaves in America. Slavery in America was a system that encompassed a wide range of occupations and roles, beyond the common stereotype of slaves as primarily agricultural laborers. While many enslaved people were indeed field hands, cooks and household servants, others worked in skilled trades, factories and in a range of other professions. These facts clearly indicate that the birth of America was built on the backs of slaves, and their labor helped establish our country as a dominant economic power. In conclusion, the growth of the slave trade and industrial complex in the 18th century was fueled by the founding fathers, laws and policies that supported the economics and practice of industrial slavery, and the financial and commercial industries that profited from it. Indeed slavery, America, and capitalism are all thriving. The connections between finance and slavery in early America are not just historical footnotes. The wealth that was generated through the exploitation of enslaved people laid the foundation for the American economy and helped to create the modern financial system in use today. The infrastructure that was built to support the slave trade, including banks, insurance companies, and shipping companies, would go on to play the crucial role in the development of the American economy in the 19th and 20th centuries.

SECTION 3: 1800-1872: ANTEBELLUM HIGHS, RECONSTRUCTION LOWS

The period between 1800 and 1872 was marked by significant highs and lows for Africans in America. At the start of the 19th century, the transatlantic slave trade was abolished, and the focus shifted to the domestic slave trade, with slaves being sold and transported within the country. The abolitionist movement gained momentum, with figures like Frederick Douglass and Harriet Tubman rising to prominence as they fought for the end of slavery. However, this period was also marked by the expansion of slavery and brutality, particularly in the southern states. The early 1800s also saw the rise of the Industrial Revolution, which increased the global demand for cotton and other agricultural products. This led to a significant increase in the number of slaves in the southern states, with cotton becoming the most important commodity in America, sustained by the captive and enslaved labor force being responsible for its production.

Over 400 slaves worked on the construction of the Capitol Building in Washington D.C.

Washington D.C., the capital of the United States, has a long history of slavery. Slavery was legal in the District of Columbia until 1862, and the city's location made it a major hub for the domestic slave trade. Enslaved people were brought to Washington D.C. from Maryland and Virginia to be sold at the slave pens and auction sites that dotted the city. The White House, which has served as the official residence of the U.S. president since 1800, was built with the labor of enslaved people. The U.S. Capitol building, which houses the legislative branch of the government, was also built with the labor of enslaved people. Slaves were rented from local slaveholders, and they worked alongside paid laborers to build the Capitol. Some estimates suggest that at least 400 slaves participated in the construction of the building. In addition to the many private slave traders, the city itself was also involved in the slave trade. The Mayor of Washington D.C. in the 1830s, William A. Bradley, was a slave trader who owned a slave pen called "The Robey House." The city also profited from the sale of enslaved people at the Central Auction Block, which was owned by the federal government.

In 1831, Nat Turner, a slave and preacher, led a rebellion against white slave owners in Virginia, resulting in the deaths of around 60 white people. The rebellion was quickly put down, and Turner was executed, along with many of his followers. In the aftermath of the rebellion, white slave owners throughout the South responded with a wave of violence and brutality towards their slaves, even those who had not been involved in the rebellion.

Aetna Insurance Company was founded in Hartford, Connecticut, in 1853. Aetna insured the lives and health of slaves as cargo on ships involved in the slave trade. The company also insured slave owners against losses due to the death or escape of their slaves, with the slave owners as the beneficiaries.

Economically in the South, plantation owners would often borrow money from merchants or banks to finance their crops and would use their slaves as collateral. If the crops failed or the owner

www.reparations-101.com | 16

was unable to pay the loan, the bank or merchant would seize the slaves and sell them to pay off the debt. Slave auctions were also used as a form of debt settlement. Slave traders would buy slaves at a reduced price from debtors and then sell them at a profit.

During this period, there were also several laws passed that further institutionalized slavery and white supremacy, including the Fugitive Slave Act of 1850 and the Dred Scott decision of 1857. These laws denied African Americans basic human rights and made it legal for slave owners to pursue and capture runaway slaves, even if they had escaped to free states. Money and profit are again the motivating and instigating factors because in addition to being used as fiduciary collateral, slaves were also used as currency in gambling. In cities such as New Orleans, Charleston and Atlanta, these enslaved humans were bought and sold at auction houses and were also used as prizes in lotteries and other games of chance, even exchanged as wedding gifts and Christmas presents. This further dehumanized and objectified African people, by reducing them to nothing more than commodities, Black people were in effect "money."

At this time enslaved people were also widely used in the logging, mining and railroad industries. In the logging industry, slaves were used to clear land, cut down trees, and transport logs to mills. They often worked in dangerous conditions, using axes and saws to chop down trees and then transporting them on rafts or barges. Enslaved people were also involved in the production of turpentine, which was a common household and industrial product in the 19th century. Today, Weyerhaeuser, is one of the largest timber companies in the world, can trace its roots back to the 19th century and their enormous profits made using enslaved laborers in the forests of Mississippi and Louisiana.

In the mining industry, enslaved people were used to extract a variety of resources including gold, silver, copper, and coal. In the gold and silver mines of the southern Appalachians, slaves often worked alongside white laborers and were subjected to dangerous conditions, including cave-ins and toxic fumes. In the copper mines of the Southwest, Native Americans and enslaved people were often used to extract the metal. One example is Tennessee Coal, Iron, and Railroad Company: This company was founded in 1852 and was one of the largest producers of iron and steel in the United States. It relied heavily on slave labor in its mines and on its railroads. In the railroad industry, enslaved people were used to construct and maintain the tracks and other infrastructure. They often worked long hours in dangerous conditions, using shovels, picks, and other tools to dig and level the ground. They also loaded and unloaded freight, and many worked as brakemen and engineers. Thousands of miles of track originally laid by slaves are operated by modern corporations including Union Pacific CSX and Norfolk Southern are still in use today.

Enslaved people were essential to the development of these industries and played a critical role in the growth of the American economy. However, their contributions were rarely acknowledged or compensated, and they were often subjected to brutal working conditions and violence. Other enslaved people worked in manufacturing, particularly in the textile industry. In the early 19th century, many textile mills in the North relied heavily on slave labor, particularly in the spinning and weaving of cotton. This practice continued even after the North abolished slavery, with some Southern plantation owners sending their slaves to work in Northern mills. Enslaved people also worked in transportation, both on land and at sea. Many worked as teamsters, driving wagons and carts, while others worked as sailors, performing a variety of tasks on ships. In fact, the slave trade itself was a significant source of employment for slaves, as many were employed in the transport and sale of other slaves.

In addition to these occupations, many slaves were also employed in skilled trades such as Blacksmithing, carpentry and bricklaying, and overall, the experience of slavery in America was far more varied than many people realize, with enslaved people occupying a wide range of roles and performing a diverse array of tasks.

SENECA VILLAGE, Upper Manhattan 1830's

Systemic and legal government abuses against Africans also continue unabated. One of the earliest recorded cases of eminent domain abuse in the United States is New York's Seneca Village. Seneca Village, a predominantly Black community in Manhattan founded in the 1820s with schools, churches, and businesses, was a thriving settlement. In the 1850s, the city used eminent domain to seize the land and displace the residents to make way for the construction of Central Park. The residents were not given fair compensation, and the displacement led to the erasure of a significant piece of Black history and culture in New York City.

www.reparations-101.com | 18

The Civil War broke out in 1861, with the Union fighting to end slavery and the Confederacy fighting to preserve it. During the American Civil War, both the Union and Confederate armies relied heavily on the labor of African Americans, but their roles and treatment differed greatly. Approximately 180,000 Black men served in the Union Army, with 40,000 losing their lives in the conflict whereas, Black people mostly served in support roles in the Confederate army and were not issued weapons. During his famous march to the sea, General William T. Sherman issued Special Field Order No. 15 in January 1865, promised 40 acres of land to each freedman and established settlements on the coast of Georgia and South Carolina for newly emancipated African Americans. The order aimed to provide land to those who had been enslaved and allow them to establish their own self-sufficient communities. However, slave owning President Andrew Johnson overturned the order later that year, and the land was returned to its former owners, leaving many formerly enslaved Black people without the resources to establish themselves as independent farmers.

The Union victory in 1865 led to the passage of the 13th Amendment, which after 246 years abolished slavery throughout the United States. Reconstruction followed, with the aim of rebuilding the country and ensuring equal rights for all citizens, including African Americans.

However, Reconstruction was short-lived, with the emergence of white supremacist groups like the Ku Klux Klan using violence and intimidation to suppress African American rights and restore white dominance. The Compromise of 1877 effectively ended Reconstruction, and the Jim Crow era began, with African Americans facing further widespread discrimination and segregation by the legal doctrine established in the 1896 Supreme Court case Plessy v. Ferguson, which upheld a Louisiana law requiring "separate but equal" facilities for whites and Black people on trains. Despite the end of slavery, the legacy of institutionalized racism and oppression continued to shape the experiences of African Americans in America.

SECTION 4: 1870–1950: AMERICAN APARTHEID

Following the Civil War, the Reconstruction era saw a brief period of progress and hope for African Americans in the South. However, with the end of Reconstruction in 1877, Jim Crow laws began to take hold, stripping away many of the rights that had been granted to Black citizens.This can accurately be called the

The chain gang ushers in the prison industrial complex.

"American Apartheid" era; a time when while technically no longer slaves, Black Americans were still not free to participate in the full measure of America's bounty which they more than helped to create. These laws included segregation, disenfranchisement, and the use of violence to maintain white supremacy. In addition to legal oppression, Black Americans also faced economic exploitation during this time. Vagrancy laws, which made it illegal to be unemployed or homeless, were used to target and imprison Black people. Once incarcerated, these individuals were often subjected to forced labor, sometimes on behalf of private companies such as the infamous Alabama-based mining company, Pratt Consolidated Coal Company. The use of forced labor in the prison system would continue well into the 20th century, eventually becoming an integral part of the prison industrial complex. This system, which disproportionately affects people of color, is described as the use of incarceration as a form of social control and profit-making.

Widespread terrorism against Blacks was pervasive at this time as lynchings and other forms of racial violence were commonplace, and African Americans were mostly denied access to education, housing, and

job opportunities. Many were forced to work in low-paying, exploitative jobs, including sharecropping, which kept them in a state of perpetual debt and poverty. One of many such events is The Tulsa Race Massacre of 1921, a violent and devastating attack on the Black community of Tulsa, Oklahoma. Seventeen years before Germany's Kristallnacht, a white mob attacked and destroyed the prosperous Black neighborhood of Greenwood, also known as "Black Wall Street." The attack resulted in the deaths of an estimated 300 Black people, displacement of thousands and the destruction of over 35 blocks of businesses and homes. The event was largely ignored and covered up for decades, and reparations have yet to be paid to the survivors and descendants of the massacre.

This era also saw the beginning of the Tuskegee syphilis experiment; a heinous medical study conducted between 1932 and 1972 by the United States Public Health Service (USPHS) and the Centers for Disease Control and Prevention (CDC). The study was designed to investigate the natural progression of untreated syphilis in African American men in rural Alabama. The study was conducted without informed consent, as the participants were not informed of the nature of the study, nor were they provided with appropriate medical treatment. Instead, they were given placebos and ineffective treatments, even when effective treatment became available. As a result of the study, many of the participants suffered from severe health consequences, including blindness, deafness, and premature death. The Tuskegee syphilis experiment became a symbol of the unethical treatment of African Americans by the government and medical establishment, and it remains a controversial and tragic episode in American history.

Despite these horrors and many others, these former slaves continued to believe in the promise of America and made significant contributions to American culture and industry during this time, developing and inventing many of the things Americans take for granted today including the rotary lawn mower, the turn signal in your car and refrigerated trucks. These newly free Black people also had time to create the country's first indigenous art forms, Jazz and the Blues, which became important cultural touchstones that reflected the experiences of African Americans during this period.

An unmitigated atrocity, the Tuskegee syphilis experiment from 1932 to 1972.

Overall, the era from 1870 to 1950 was marked by both oppression and Jim Crow for Black Americans. Despite facing legal and economic barriers, they continued to push for equal rights and to make important contributions to American culture. However, the legacy of this era, including the prison industrial complex and ongoing systemic racism, continues to have an impact on Black communities today.

SECTION 5: 1950-2008: CIVIL RIGHTS? MORAL WRONGS

The mid-twentieth century was a period of considerable progress and intense struggles for African Americans. The Civil Rights Movement, led by Martin Luther King Jr. and Malcolm X, was at its peak, demanding an end to segregation and systemic racism. While the Brown v. Board of Education case in 1954 declared segregation unconstitutional, the reality was different. Governor George Wallace

Gov. George Wallace blocks Black students from entering the University of Alabama in 1963

infamously stood in the schoolhouse door to block two Black students from entering the University of Alabama in 1963. In general, African Americans were still facing discrimination in all aspects of life, including housing, education, and employment. Malcolm X and King advocated different approaches to the fight for equality, with Malcolm X's advocacy for self-defense and Black nationalism in contrast to King's message of nonviolence and social integration. However, progress like the passage of the Voting Rights Act in 1965 was hindered by events such as the nationwide riots after the assassination of Martin Luther King in April of 1968 and the Rodney King beating by the LAPD in 1991, and subsequent acquittal of the officers involved, sparking more riots in Los Angeles. The War on Drugs, which disproportionately affected Black communities, also led to the rise of crack cocaine and the crack epidemic. The urban crack epidemic of the 1980s was a devastating public health crisis that disproportionately affected African American communities across the United States. Crack cocaine, a highly addictive and potent form of cocaine that could be smoked, was introduced to urban areas in the early 1980s and quickly spread throughout low-income neighborhoods. The epidemic led to a surge in drug-related crime and violence, which further devastated already politically disenfranchised, economically and educationally disadvantaged inner city neighborhoods. Additionally, there is evidence to suggest that the Central Intelligence Agency (CIA) played a significant role in the spread of crack cocaine in African American communities through its involvement in the Iran-Contra affair. According to multiple investigations and testimonies, the CIA worked with urban drug dealers, including

Rodney King beating by LAPD in 1991

notorious figure "Freeway" Rick Ross, to smuggle cocaine into the United States and sell it in African American neighborhoods, thereby financing the Contra rebels, who were major cocaine traffickers and part time CIA backed "freedom" fighters. Tens of thousands of weapons and millions of rounds of ammunition were also let loose against the people of Black America through this government backed operation.

The urban crack epidemic had devastating consequences for African American communities, including mass incarceration, broken families, and economic decline. While over-policing of Black neighborhoods became a means of revenue generation for states, cities and counties resulting in the mass incarceration of Black men through draconian laws and aggressive over policing like the "Three Strikes" laws, "Stop and Frisk" and the devastating "94 Crime Bill." Companies such as the Corrections Corporation of America (CCA) and GEO Group, are among those that have profited billions and supercharged the prison industrial complex around the country.

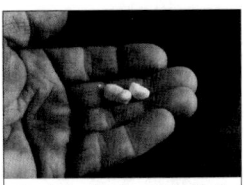
Crack cocaine devastates Black America in the 1990's

Affirmative action, which aimed to increase diversity and equal opportunities for marginalized groups, also faced challenges from those who saw it as reverse discrimination, and soon the progress of the civil rights movement was countered by a growing conservative movement, which argued that the country had achieved a "post-racial" society, and that affirmative action and other measures aimed at promoting diversity were no longer necessary, leading to successful challenges and rollbacks of Affirmative action in university admissions and minority hiring across the country.

Overall, the period from 1950 to 2008 was marked by noteworthy but superficial progress and continued struggles for African Americans, with victories in the civil rights movement and advancements in culture and technology. However, these advancements were generally met with resistance leaving systemic racism and discrimination firmly entrenched in American life. Of example is the replacement of African American civil rights icon, Supreme Court Justice Thurgood Marshall with the conservative and GOP backed African American Clarence Thomas who has consistently voted against the interest of Black Americans in his tenure on the bench even as he can arguably be the most prominent example of the affirmative action policies he voted to end.

SECTION 6: 2008 -2023 POST – RACIAL?

In 2008, Barack Obama made history by becoming the first Black President of the United States. His presidency was marked by the slogan "Yes We Can" and brought a sense of hope and change to many Americans.

However, despite Obama's victory and his efforts to push for policies that promoted racial equality, the idea of a "post-racial" America was far from reality. Obama's presidency was met with a backlash from some white Americans who believed that the election of a Black President meant that racism was no longer a problem. This sentiment was fueled by right-wing media outlets, such as FOX News, which challenged his birth status, often criticized Obama and portrayed him as Muslim and "un-American". During Obama's second term, the Black Lives Matter movement emerged in response to the police killings of unarmed Black people, such as Mike Brown in Ferguson, Missouri. The movement called attention to the systemic racism and police brutality faced by Black Americans. In addition to police violence, the Flint water crisis in 2014 exposed the environmental racism faced by Black communities. The crisis began when the city of Flint, Michigan, switched its water source to the Flint River, which was contaminated with lead. The predominantly Black community was left with toxic water and inadequate government response. Despite the so called progress made towards racial equality, the election of Donald Trump in 2016 marked a significant setback for the movement. Trump's campaign was driven by a swaggering racist and xenophobic rhetoric, and his policies, such as the travel ban on Muslim-majority countries, and draconian anti-immigration measures further perpetuated discrimination.

In conclusion, the period from 2008 to 2023 was marked by both progress and setbacks in the fight for racial equality. The election of Barack Obama represented a historic moment, but the backlash and continued systemic racism revealed that the idea of a "post-racial" America was far from reality. The Black Lives Matter movement and the Flint water crisis brought attention to the ongoing struggles faced by Black communities, while the election of Donald Trump highlighted the persistent presence of racism and xenophobia in American politics.

Contaminated water in Flint, Michigan

The history of African Americans in the United States is a long and painful one, marked by centuries of systemic oppression, exploitation and violence. From the arrival of the first enslaved Africans on the continent in 1619 to the present day, Black people have endured countless atrocities at the hands of government, corporations and society at large in a seamless and unbroken timeline. Slavery, apartheid, lynching, redlining, police brutality, mass incarceration and environmental racism are just a few examples of the many forms of discrimination and violence that Black people have and continue to face throughout American history. Today, despite some "progress" in civil rights and racial equality, systemic racism flourishes and continues to plague American society.

CHAPTER 2

THE IMPACT: ECONOMICS IN BLACK AND WHITE

Having established a reliable history of facts and events; let us now discuss the economic impact of slavery and racism on Black Americans and the lasting and generational effect that can still be felt today. Let it be said that slavery can indeed be accurately called "the big bang" of capitalism as the origins of modern capitalism can be traced back to the transatlantic slave trade, which began in the 16th century and lasted until the 19th century. European powers established colonial outposts in the Americas and elsewhere, primarily for the purpose of exploiting natural resources and labor. The slave trade enabled plantation owners to access a vast pool of inexpensive labor, which helped drive the production of agricultural commodities, such as sugar, tobacco and cotton, and enabled the growth of industries such as shipping and the commercial financial markets.

Chattel slavery was indeed the catalyzing human element in capitalism's "holy trinity" of land, labor and natural resources, and the exploitation of kidnapped and enslaved people accelerated the rise of the modern economy. Capitalism is defined as an economic system in which private individuals or companies own and operate the means of production and distribution of goods and services for profit; and the exploitation of slave labor and the trade in slave-produced commodities no doubt established the foundations of today's modern banking and finance industries. To finance the purchase of slaves and fund the building of plantations, European merchants and investors established some of the earliest modern banks and investment funds. The sale and trade of enslaved Africans created a lucrative commodity market, which in turn drove the development of modern commodity and futures markets. In addition, the insurance industry developed in order to provide coverage for the loss of slave ships and human cargo, which was a significant risk in this era. It cannot be overlooked that the slave trade was intimately connected to the global economy, and millions of kidnapped and enslaved Africans were often used as collateral in international trade. European merchants would use enslaved Africans as collateral to secure loans to finance the slave trade without passion or hesitation. This practice extended to the United States, where enslaved Africans were used as collateral for loans from European banks. As proof of concept, many of these original companies including Barclays, The Royal Bank of Scotland and Lloyd's of London are well known and exist to this day.

The profits generated by the slave trade and the wealth it created were reinvested In other sectors of the economy, such as manufacturing and industry, creating a ripple effect that further accelerated the growth of capitalism. The slave trade also provided an abundant source of raw materials like cotton and tobacco for factories in Europe and America, allowing manufacturers to produce goods more cheaply and efficiently than ever before. In addition, slavery was the key factor in driving the profitability of all produced goods and commodities, and thus, played a key role in the development of new financial instruments and markets. The need to hedge against the risks of slave ownership and trade gave rise to the development of insurance and reinsurance markets. The trade in slave-produced goods, such as tobacco, sugar and cotton, helped establish commodity markets, and the sale of slave mortgages helped develop the bond market.

The infrastructure that supported the slave trade, such as ports, ships and warehouses, provided opportunities for entrepreneurial individuals to build wealth and invest in emerging industries. The wealth generated from the slave trade helped to finance the development of factories and the expansion of industry in the United States and Europe. Moreover, the slave trade created a labor market that helped to drive down wages and maintain a system of economic inequality that persists to this day. The legacy of slavery can be seen in the disparities in wealth, income and access to education and opportunities that continue to plague communities of color (around the world) today.

The generational impact of slavery and racism on Black Americans can be seen in the lack of intergenerational wealth transfer. White Americans are more able to pass down assets and wealth to their children, providing them with a financial cushion and opportunities for upward mobility. Conversely, due to the historical denial of wealth-building opportunities for Black Americans, they have not been able to accumulate the same level of intergenerational wealth transfer. The economic impact of slavery and racism on Black Americans is not just a matter of historical injustice, but a continuing issue that requires acknowledgement and action.

... ON THE OTHER HAND...

The generational economic benefits of slavery and racism on white Americans are deeply intertwined with the history of the United States. For centuries, white Americans have benefited from the exploitation of African Americans, by forced labor, theft of land and denial of equal access to economic opportunities. From Brooks Brothers who made fine clothes for the plantation class and uniforms for their slaves to the tobacco rich Duke family of North Carolina to banking magnates like JP Morgan and Harriman Brothers; the history is full of fortunes made by the white capitalists of the day, but we know that is just the beginning. One significant way that white Americans continue to benefit economically from this legacy is through corporations and their 401k's and stock portfolios. Many major corporations in the United States were built on the backs of enslaved Africans or through the exploitation of Black labor during Jim Crow segregation. As a result, these companies have accumulated vast amounts of wealth that have been passed down through generations of white families. In addition, policies such as redlining, which systematically denied Black Americans access to housing and other resources, helped to create, and maintain wealth disparities between Black and white Americans. This allowed white families to accumulate wealth through homeownership and other investments, while denying those same opportunities to Black families. The economic benefits of racism and slavery also continue to be reflected in the vast disparities in income and wealth between Black and white Americans today. According to a 2020 report by the Brookings Institution, the median white family had a net worth of $171,000 in 2016, while the median Black family had a net worth of just $17,150: a factor of roughly ten times. This wealth gap is largely the result of centuries of historical economic injustices that have limited opportunities for Black Americans to accumulate wealth and pass it down to future generations.

CHAPTER 3

REPARATIONS: WHAT ARE THEY? WHO GETS THEM? WHO PAYS? AND WHY?

Having established a reliable and accurate history of events and their toxic side effects; The next step is to adopt a common definition and concept of exactly what reparations are and if African Americans qualify?

Reparations are payments made by a government or corporation to compensate individuals or groups for harm or damage caused by past wrongs or injustices. In order to establish a case for human rights reparations, several conditions must be met. These include:

1. The existence of a systematic violation of human rights: There must be evidence of a widespread and systematic violation of human rights, such as torture, forced labor, genocide or crimes against humanity. The case for reparations for slavery in the United States is based in the fact that millions of Africans were killed, kidnapped, enslaved and forced to work under brutal conditions for generations with no political franchise, economic recourses or mobility. This is widely covered in Chapter 1.

2. The recognition of responsibility: The perpetrators of the human rights abuses must be recognized as being responsible for the harm caused.

3. The existence of victims: There must be identifiable victims who have suffered harm as a result of human rights abuses.

4. The obligation to provide remedy.

Recognition of responsibility states that the perpetrators of the human rights abuses must be recognized as being responsible for the harm caused. In the case of slavery, this responsibility rests with the slave traders, slave owners and the institutions and governments that supported and profited from the slave trade. In America, the responsibility for the harm caused by slavery and the slave trade rests with many individuals, institutions and governments. In addition, numerous banks and insurance companies profited from the slave trade, including JPMorgan Chase, Bank of America, Aetna, and New York Life which have all acknowledged their ties to slavery, and have made mostly token efforts towards reparations. On a larger scale, the US Federal Government supported and benefited from slavery through policies such as the "Fugitive Slave Act" and the "Three-Fifths Compromise." Many states, particularly in the South, also had laws that upheld slavery and racial segregation, including Jim Crow laws that discriminated against Black Americans even long after slavery was legally abolished. It is essential to recognize the responsibility of these entities in perpetuating slavery and the slave trade to fully understand the need for reparations for the harm caused to African Americans. Throughout American history, there have been notable figures who held the highest office in the land, but behind their leadership and achievements lies a dark truth.

Many of the presidents who shaped the nation were also slaveowners, perpetuating the institution of slavery while simultaneously proclaiming the values of freedom and equality. From George Washington to Thomas Jefferson, James Madison to James Monroe, and numerous others, these "slaveowners-in-chief" played a significant role in shaping the early development of the United States. Their actions, decisions, and legacy are complex and controversial, raising important questions about the contradictions within the fabric of American democracy.

SLAVEOWNERS-IN-CHIEF

Many American presidents were slave owners, including:

George Washington **(owned hundreds of slaves)**

Thomas Jefferson **(owned over 600 slaves)**

James Madison **(owned over 100 slaves)**

James Monroe **(owned hundreds of slaves)**

Andrew Jackson **(owned over 100 slaves)**

Martin Van Buren **(owned one slave)**

William Henry Harrison **(owned eleven slaves)**

John Tyler **(owned slaves, but the exact number is unclear)**

James K. Polk **(owned about 20 slaves)**

Zachary Taylor **(owned over 100 slaves)**

Andrew Johnson **(owned slaves, but the exact number is unclear)**

It is worth noting that several slave owning U.S. presidents were also integral to the institution of higher education in America. Slavery played a significant role in shaping higher education in America. Many of the nation's oldest and most prestigious universities, including Harvard, Yale, Princeton, and Columbia, were founded during the colonial era and relied on the enormous profits from the slave industrial complex for their construction, maintenance, and operation. Dozens of prominent universities were founded by slave-owning individuals or with funding from the slave economy and built by the hands, blood, bone and backs of enslaved Africans. They laid the roots for what would become America's slave industrial education complex.

AMERICAN SLAVE INDUSTRIAL EDUCATION COMPLEX

These universities often had close ties to slaveholders, and the wealth generated by slavery allowed many families to endow chairs, fund buildings, and provide financial support for these institutions. Slave owning Presidents Thomas Jefferson, James Madison, and George Washington to name a few were all involved in the founding of universities and colleges. They believed that education was essential for the development of a democratic society, but only for a select few. The education of white, male elites was prioritized, while the education of enslaved and free Black people was discouraged or outright banned.

While these universities have mostly sought to distance themselves from their connections to slavery, their legacies continue to be felt. One of the most significant ways in which this legacy manifests itself is in the lack of Black students at these universities. Despite years of token affirmative action policies and diversity initiatives, many of these institutions remain overwhelmingly white, with low levels of enrollment among African American students. For example, in 2019, the undergraduate student body at the University of Virginia, built on land that was once part of Jefferson's plantation, was only 6.3% Black, despite the fact that Black people make up over 19% of the state's population. At Georgetown, only 6% of the undergraduate student body is Black, compared to the university's historical ties to the slave trade and its role in selling enslaved people to maintain its financial stability. The lack of Black students at all the Universities that make up the American slave industrial education complex is not just a matter of historical legacy, but also a reflection of ongoing structural inequality in higher education. Many of these schools have high tuition costs and limited financial aid, which can make them unaffordable for low-income students, who are disproportionately Black and brown. Additionally, many of these institutions have long histories of discrimination and exclusion, which can make them feel unwelcoming or hostile to Black students. It should be noted that some of these universities have taken steps to acknowledge and research their ties to slavery, and many have established initiatives to promote dialogue and understanding of their historical connections to slavery.

To truly address the legacy of slavery corporations, governments and universities must not only acknowledge their past ties to the slave economy but also actively work to address the ongoing inequalities that result from that history.

The existence of victims: There must be identifiable victims who have suffered harm as a result of human rights abuses. In the case of slavery, the victims are the descendants of enslaved Africans who continue to suffer from the intergenerational effects of slavery, including economic, social, and psychological harm. 2020 census records approximately 37 million in this population.

The obligation to provide remedy: The perpetrators of the human rights abuses have an obligation to provide a remedy to the victims. This seems to be a point of contention as many Americans may reject the notion of their personal responsibility or simply see reparations for African Americans as a radical and impossible fantasy. However, it must be noted that many other countries have made efforts to address historical wrongs through reparations. Reparations can take different forms, including financial compensation, educational programs, and policy changes aimed at redressing the harm caused by historical injustices, acknowledging the historical and ongoing impact of such crimes on affected communities.

IS THERE A PRECEDENT FOR THIS? ABSOLUTELY!

Germany signed the Luxembourg agreements with Jewish holocaust survivors in 1953. Paying them billions for human rights abuses suffered during World War II.

The 1953 Germany settlement with Israel and Jewish Holocaust survivors, commonly known as the Luxembourg Agreement, was a significant reparation agreement aimed at providing compensation to Holocaust survivors and the newly established state of Israel for the crimes committed by Nazi Germany during World War II. The agreement was reached in Luxembourg on September 10, 1952, and was signed by representatives from the Federal Republic of Germany, Israel, and the Claims Conference.

Under the agreement, Germany agreed to make payments to Israel and the Claims Conference, which acted as the representative of Jewish Holocaust survivors. The payments were intended to provide compensation for the suffering, losses, and property seizures endured by Jewish individuals and communities during the Holocaust. The agreement included provisions for various types of compensation, including individual reparations, indemnification for the state of Israel, and funds for the Claims Conference to support Holocaust survivors.

The specific details of the settlement include:

- **Total Amount:** Germany agreed to pay a total of 3 billion German marks (equivalent to approximately 845 million US dollars at the time) to Israel and the Claims Conference over a period of 14 years.

Belgian King Philippe apologizes in the Congo 2013

- **Individual Reparations:** Germany made direct payments to Holocaust survivors, prioritizing those who suffered the most severe persecution and losses during the Nazi regime.

- **Indemnification to Israel:** Germany provided funds to support the absorption and rehabilitation of Holocaust survivors in Israel, as well as for the construction of infrastructure and institutions.

- **Payments to the Claims Conference:** The Claims Conference received funds to assist Holocaust survivors worldwide, including medical and social services, Holocaust education and research, and the recovery of Jewish-owned assets.

In addition, the German government established the "Remembrance, Responsibility, and Future" foundation (officially known as "Stiftung Erinnerung, Verantwortung und Zukunft") in 2000. The foundation collected funds from German companies that had profited from or utilized forced labor during the war. These funds were used to compensate victims of forced labor. The foundation disbursed over €4.4 billion (euros) to more than 1.6 million victims of forced labor. BMW paid 43 million euros, Krups paid 41 million euros, Volkswagen paid 16 million euros, Siemens paid 50 million euros, and Deutsche Bank paid 10 million euros. Other German companies also made contributions to the fund.

Apart from the "Remembrance, Responsibility, and Future" foundation, there have been other instances of German companies providing reparations to Holocaust survivors. For example, in the 1990s, several Swiss banks were found to have held assets belonging to Holocaust victims. After legal proceedings, the banks agreed to pay $1.25 billion in restitution to the victims and their heirs.

In 2013, the British government issued a formal apology and paid a settlement to thousands of Kenyan citizens who were tortured and abused during the Mau Mau uprising in the 1950s. The British government had previously denied responsibility for the abuses, but the settlement was seen as a recognition of their complicity.

Another example is the case of the Belgian government's payment of reparations to victims of its colonization of Congo. In 2020, the Belgian king expressed his "deepest regrets" for the brutal colonization of Congo and pledged to work towards reconciliation. The Belgian government also set up a fund to support the Congolese people and announced plans to return some stolen artifacts to Congo.

Even more examples of international governments that have made reparations payments include:

1. France has acknowledged its role in the slave trade and has made some efforts towards reparations, including the establishment of a National Day of Remembrance for slavery and its abolition.

2. In 1988, the US government has made reparations payments to 120,000 Japanese American survivors of internment camps during World War II.

3. In the aftermath of apartheid, the South African government established the Truth and Reconciliation Commission, which provided reparations to victims of human rights violations. These reparations included financial compensation, educational opportunities, and health care services.

4. In 2016, the Canadian government announced a $8.9 million settlement with Indigenous survivors of the "Sixties Scoop," a practice in which Indigenous children were forcibly removed from their families and placed in non-indigenous homes. The settlement included individual payments to survivors and funding for cultural support programs.

In conclusion, reparations are payments made by a government or corporation to compensate individuals or groups for harm or damage caused by past wrongs or injustices. The case for reparations for African Americans is based on the widespread and systematic violation of human rights through slavery and its legacy, the recognition of responsibility of individuals, institutions, and governments, the existence of victims who have suffered harm because of human rights abuses and the obligation to provide remedy. While there may be resistance to the idea of reparations, it is important to recognize the precedent set by other countries and historical examples of reparations, and to acknowledge the ongoing impact of historical injustices on affected communities.

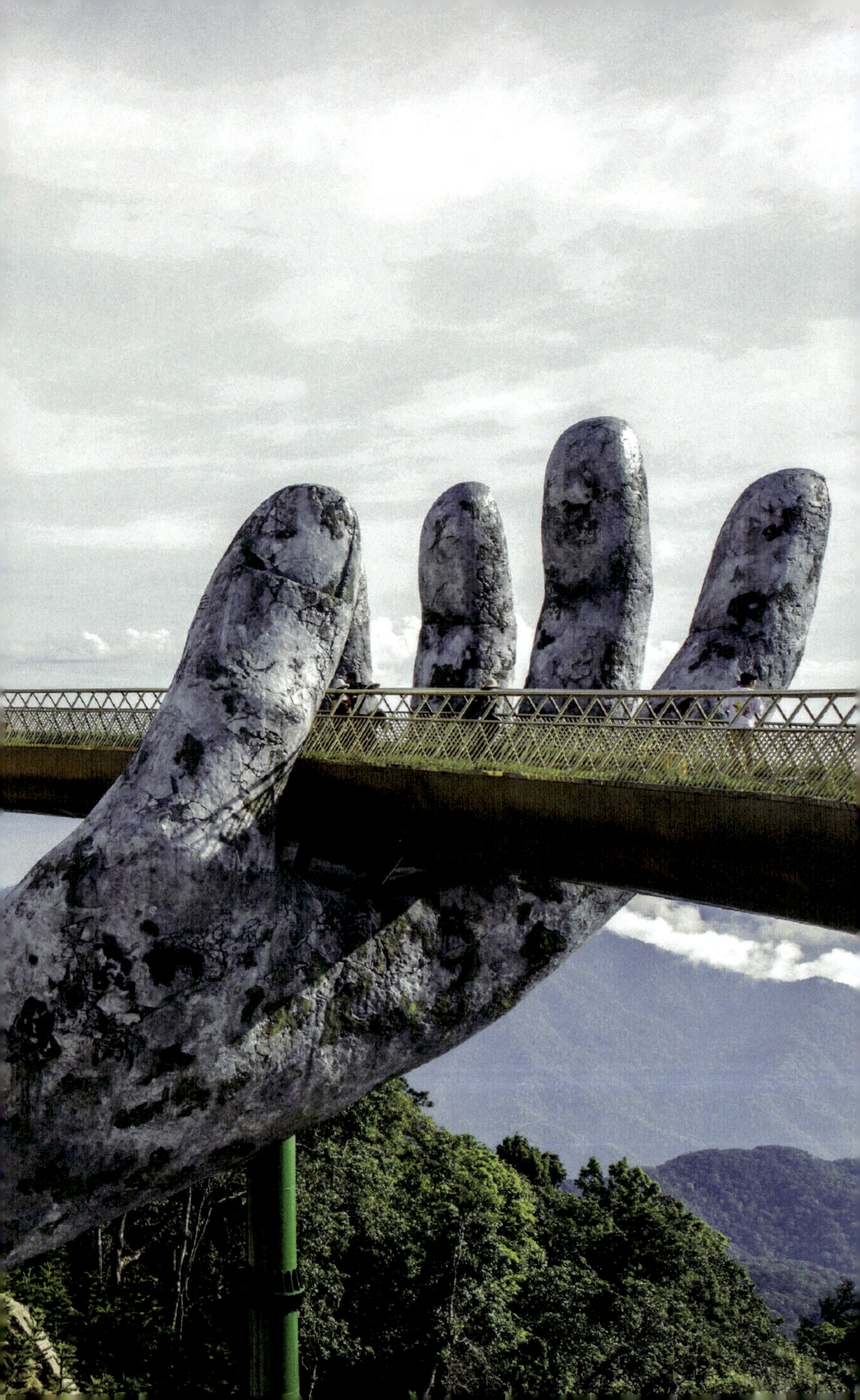

CHAPTER 4

THE REMEDY: THE CASE FOR FINANCIAL COMPENSATION AS A FORM OF REPARATIONS

The issue of reparations for African Americans has been a controversial topic for decades. Many argue that reparations would be too costly or impractical, while others argue that it is necessary to address the ongoing effects of slavery and systemic racism. In this chapter, we will explore the case for financial compensation as a form of reparations. One of the main arguments for financial compensation as a form of reparations is that money was the root cause and key benefit of the enslavement and exploitation of African Americans. The transatlantic slave trade and the forced labor of enslaved Africans were driven by economic gain, and the profits from slavery helped to build the American economy. It is estimated that the unpaid labor of enslaved Africans alone is worth trillions of dollars in today's currency.

In addition to the economic benefits of slavery, African Americans have also faced systemic discrimination and racism that has led to economic disadvantage. This includes practices such as redlining, which denied Black families access to housing loans, and discrimination in employment and education. Financial compensation would not only help to address the economic impact of slavery and systemic racism but would also serve as a form of acknowledgement and recognition of the harm that has been done. It would help to create a more just and equitable society by providing a pathway to economic stability and opportunity for African Americans.

www.reparations-101.com | 44

There are several models for how financial compensation could be provided as a form of reparations. One option is direct cash payments to individuals or families who can prove their ancestors were enslaved. This would require extensive research and documentation, but it would provide a tangible benefit to those who have been directly impacted by slavery. Another option is to invest in programs that support education, housing and economic development for African American communities. This could include funding for historically Black colleges and universities, affordable housing initiatives and small business development programs.

Overall, financial compensation as a form of reparations is a necessary step towards acknowledging and addressing the harm caused by slavery and systemic racism and more importantly disconnect the capitalistic benefits of systemic racism. While there are challenges to implementing such a program, the benefits of creating a more just and equitable society far outweigh the costs. It is time for America to take responsibility for its past, and work towards a more equitable future.

THE REMEDY: WHO PAYS – THE DIRTY DOZEN

Industrial scale slavery also played a significant role in the development of modern finance.

Slave owners used slaves as collateral for loans, and slave markets served as a source of liquidity for the buying and selling of slaves. This helped establish the foundations of modern banking and finance including the insurance industry and the commodity, stock and bond markets which continue to shape the global economy today. The following 12 companies are some of the oldest, most well-known and profitable corporations in the world. They all have a dark and blood-stained history rooted in the slave trade and slavery in America. Without exception, they are the crucible of American capitalism as we know it today. They are also the financial cornerstone of the slave industrial complex:

- **JP Morgan Chase & Co.,** one of the Federal Reserve's founding banks and one of the largest banks in the United States traces its roots to two banks among others that were heavily involved in the slave trade, Chemical Bank and the Manufacturers Hanover Trust. These banks provided financing to plantation owners and slave traders, and some of their executives were slave owners themselves. JP Morgan himself owned slaves and his company, J.P. Morgan & Co., financed numerous slave plantations in the South as well as financed railroads that transported slaves and traded in Southern bonds that financed the Confederacy during the Civil War. In response, JP Morgan Chase worth 475 billion in 2021, publicly apologized for its role in the slave trade and established a $5 million scholarship fund for African American students in Louisiana.

- **Bank of America Corp.** profited from slavery through two of its predecessor banks, Bank of Metropolis, founded in 1792 in Washington DC and Richmond's Bank of Virginia founded in 1804. Both financed slave owners before and the Confederacy during the Civil War. Many of the bank's clients were plantation owners who relied on enslaved labor to run their businesses. These clients often used their enslaved people as collateral for loans, and these banks were happy to provide the credit they needed to keep their operations running. They also invested in companies that profited from slavery, such as cotton mills and sugar plantations. Furthermore, the bank's profits were then used to finance the slave trade, including the purchase of more enslaved people from Africa, fulfilling the toxic cycle of blood, misery, exploitation and profit.

- **Citibank,** also a charter bank of the Fed and one of the largest banks in the United States, has a long history that is deeply intertwined with the institution of slavery. The bank was founded in 1812 as the City Bank of New York and eventually became known as Citibank. Throughout its history, the bank has played a significant role in the slave trade and in financing the slave economy. The bank's founder, Samuel Osgood was a wealthy merchant who profited from the slave trade. In the late 1700s, he was involved in the construction and financing of ships that transported slaves from Africa to the United States. Osgood also owned a plantation in Jamaica that relied on the labor of enslaved people.

In the mid-1800s, Citibank became one of the largest banks in the United States, and it continued to play a significant role in financing the slave economy. The bank provided loans to slave owners and to businesses that profited from the slave trade.

In 1860, for example, Citibank lent more than $3 million to cotton planters in the South, who relied on enslaved labor to cultivate their crops.

After the Civil War, Citibank continued to be involved in the exploitation of African Americans. During the Reconstruction era, the bank provided loans to white landowners who used sharecropping to exploit the labor of formerly enslaved people. Citibank also invested in companies that used forced labor, including the convict leasing system, which exploited Black prisoners in the South.

In recent years, Citibank has acknowledged its history of involvement in the slave trade and has taken some steps to address this legacy. With reported total assets of approximately $1.95 trillion in December 2020, Citibank had revenue of approximately $74.3 billion and a net income of approximately $11.4 billion. Citibank announced that it would provide $1 billion in loans to help close the racial wealth gap in the United States. The bank also pledged to increase its investments in Blackowned businesses and to make changes to its hiring and promotion practices to promote diversity and inclusion.

- **Wells Fargo & Co.,** this banking institution has acknowledged that it profited from slavery through its predecessor banks, including Wachovia who traces its roots to the Georgia Railroad and Banking Company, owned slaves who were used to build railroad tracks in Georgia. The bank also acknowledged that two of its other predecessors, the Bank of Charleston founded in 1792 and the Farmers' and Exchange Bank, had accepted slaves as collateral for loans.

- **Barclays Bank PLC** was established in 1690 in London and played a significant role in financing the transatlantic slave trade investing in slaves as both cargo and property. It continued to profit from slavery even after the slave trade was abolished in 1807 by providing loans to slave traders and plantation owners. Worth an estimated 32 billion in 2021, Barclays has apologized for its role in the slave trade and set up a $5 million slavery and remembrance fund.

- **Brown Brothers Harriman & Co.,** also key player in the creation of the Federal Reserve System is a leading and privately held investment bank was founded in 1818 by the Brown and Harriman families, with many of BBH's early clients, like them were slave owners and plantation owners in the American South. The bank provided financing and other financial services to these clients, enabling them to expand their operations and acquire more slaves. The Brown family's wealth and influence grew steadily over the years, and by the mid-1800s, they had become one of the most prominent financiers of the slave trade. BBH was one of the earliest and largest investors in Southern cotton, which was produced by slave labor. The bank helped finance the purchase of plantations and slaves, and then provided financial services to the plantation owners, such as loans, currency exchanges, and sales of cotton to textile mills in the North and in Europe. The family's investment bank, Brown Brothers Harriman, was one of the top financiers of the Confederacy during the Civil War and played a crucial role in providing the South with the funds it needed to continue fighting while simultaneously helping to finance the Union Army as well. This lesser known but powerful institution has been involved in shaping many significant events in American financial history with billions and billions paid in African blood and misery. Today, BBH is still in operation as a private investment bank and wealth management firm, with headquarters in New York City. While the bank has publicly acknowledged its historical ties to slavery and has taken some steps towards reparations, some critics argue that more needs to be done to address the bank's past and ongoing complicity in systems of oppression.

- **Bank of New York Mellon Corporation,** is one of the largest financial institutions in the United States. According to its most recent financial statements, as of December 31, 2021, the bank had total assets of $503.8 billion and has a controversial history with regards to its connection to the slave trade and slave industrial complex.

    In the 1800s, Mellon Bank's predecessor, T. Mellon & Sons, was a prominent financial institution in the city of Pittsburgh. According to historical records, the Mellon family owned over 1,000 slaves and made their fortune through investments in industries that were connected to the slave trade, such as cotton, tobacco, and railroads. Thomas Mellon, the founder of the bank, was known to have owned shares in a steamship company that transported slaves from Africa to the Americas. The Mellon family's ties to the slave industrial complex did not end there. Andrew Mellon, the bank's namesake, served as Secretary of the Treasury under three presidents in the 1920s and was a major proponent of tax cuts and deregulation that benefited the wealthy elite, many of whom inherited their wealth from the slave trade.

- **Lloyd's of London,** the world's leading insurance market, provided insurance policies to slave traders and slave ship owners, covering the loss of human cargo during transportation across the Atlantic. Lloyd's also insured slave plantations and their crops against losses due to natural disasters or slave uprisings.

- **New York Life Insurance Co.,** founded in 1845 also sold policies on the lives of slaves, paying out claims to their owners when they died. The company continued to profit from these policies even after the end of the Civil War. Throughout its history, New York Life has faced various controversies related to race and discrimination. In the early 20th century, the company was accused of discriminating against Black policyholders by charging them higher premiums than white policyholders. In 1973, the company was sued by the NAACP for allegedly refusing to hire Black employees and for discriminatory practices in the workplace. Today New York Life is one of the largest life insurance companies in the world, with over $700 billion in assets under management.

- **Aetna Inc.** now a subsidiary of CVS Health and one of the largest insurance companies in the United States, Aetna Insurance Company was founded in Hartford, Connecticut, in 1853. Aetna insured the lives and health of slaves as cargo on ships involved in the slave trade. The company also insured slave owners against losses due to the death or escape of their slaves, with the slave owners as the beneficiaries. This insurance company has acknowledged that it insured the lives of slaves.

- **The Hartford Financial Services Group** was founded in 1810 as The Hartford Fire Insurance Company. Its founders included three of the wealthiest men in Hartford, Connecticut, who were also among the largest slave owners in the state. These men had a significant role in the economy of the region, owning and operating numerous businesses, including textile mills, shipping companies and banks. They invested heavily in the slave trade including in the purchase and sale of slaves, as well as the production of goods using slave labor. The Hartford Fire Insurance Company insured ships engaged in the slave trade, as well as plantations that relied on slave labor. The Hartford has acknowledged that it sold policies to slave owners covering their slaves as property.

- **The Travelers Companies, Inc.** was founded in 1853 as St. Paul Fire and Marine Insurance Co. and is headquartered in New York City. It is one of the largest providers of property and casualty insurance in the United States, Travelers profited from insuring the ships that transported enslaved people across the Atlantic Ocean during the transatlantic slave trade. The company also insured slave owners and their property including slaves, as well as the products of slave labor, such as tobacco and cotton. Additionally, Travelers invested in Southern railroads and other businesses that relied on slave labor. Later in the 20th century, the company provided coverage for employers who discriminated against African American workers and charged higher premiums to African American policyholders and denied coverage to African American-owned businesses. Travelers is currently ranked as the second largest commercial property and casualty insurance company in the United States, with a market cap of over $40 billion.

Obviously, it is important to hold these companies accountable for their past actions and demand reparations for the profits they accumulated through slavery and its legacy. But there are many others across the Fortune 500 to share in being held accountable and making financial amends, including:

Deere & Co. profited from the slave labor used in the production of cotton.

Royal Bank of Scotland Group PLC has a history of benefiting from slavery, with its roots going back to the Bank of Scotland which engaged in financing plantations in the West Indies in the 18th century, investing in slaves as both cargo and property. The bank continued to profit from slavery until the abolition of slavery in the British Empire in 1833.

Eli Lilly and Co. profited from the slave labor used in the production of cotton.

The Chubb Corporation. One of the largest property and casualty insurance companies in the world, with a strong presence in the United States. The company has acknowledged that it provided insurance coverage for slave owners in the 1800s and has also acknowledged its involvement in discriminatory practices during the 20th century.

R.J. Reynolds Tobacco Company – This tobacco company was founded by Richard Joshua Reynolds, who made his fortune in the tobacco industry, which relied heavily on slave labor.

Norfolk Southern – This railroad company has a history of using slave labor to build its rail lines.

CSX Corp. – This transportation company has acknowledged that it profited from slavery through its predecessor, the Baltimore and Ohio Railroad.

Union Pacific Corp. – This transportation company has acknowledged that it profited from slavery through its predecessor, the Southern Pacific Railroad.

The Du Pont Corp. – This chemical company was founded by Éleuthère Irénée du Pont de Nemours, who made his fortune in the gunpowder industry, which relied heavily on slave labor.

The Procter & Gamble Company – This consumer goods company was founded by William Procter and James Gamble, who made their fortune in the soap and candle industries, which also relied heavily on slave labor.

Brooks Brothers made a fortune making suits and clothes for wealthy plantation owners and uniforms for enslaved workers.

The Southern Company used enslaved people to build and maintain their infrastructure, including power plants and dams.

Colgate-Palmolive – The company's founder, William Colgate, was a slave owner and trader.

Tiffany & Co. – This luxury jewelry and specialty retailer used to trade in slave-produced silver and cotton.

Weyerhaeuser – This timber company, one of the largest in the world, can be traced back to the 19th century. According to historian Edward E. Baptist, Weyerhaeuser "grew large and profitable through the use of enslaved laborers in the forests of Mississippi and Louisiana."

THE REMEDY: THE FORMULA

The Reparations 101 formula prescribes a 70/30 corporate/government division of payment which substantially limits the exposure of Joe Average taxpayer. To get the conversations started, the Reparations 101 proposal is a 5-8% revenue tax on these corporations and others for a period of 20-40 years. The rest would come from the federal government who also profited and bears the weight of accountability and responsibility.

WHY SHOULD GOVERNMENT PAY?

While corporations may have profited from the slave industrial complex, they are not the only ones responsible for its existence and perpetuation. Governments and the English Royal Crown played a significant role in creating and upholding the system of slavery in America and has a responsibility to take action to address its harms. Moreover, it is the government's responsibility to ensure that corporations operate ethically and in the best interests of society, and to hold them accountable for any damage they cause. Therefore, both corporations and governments must take accountability, and work together to provide just and fair compensation and restitution to slavery's victims. Additionally,

www.reparations-101.com | 52

the government has a responsibility to provide reparations for the incalculable harms caused by slavery and its ongoing effects, such as the wealth gap, housing discrimination and unequal access to education and healthcare. This responsibility is based on the recognition that these governments, through their policies and actions, have both instigated and perpetuated systemic racism and inequality that continue to affect Black Americans today.

THE FEDERAL RESERVE

The Federal Reserve System was created by the Federal Reserve Act of 1913. As uncomfortable and unpleasant it is to report, several of the charter banks that founded the Federal Reserve System have a detailed history of involvement in the slave trade and other forms of discrimination. These charter members were:

- **JPMorgan Chase:** JPMorgan Chase has a long history of connections to the slave trade, including providing loans to slave owners and accepting slaves as collateral. The bank has also been involved in other forms of discrimination, such as redlining, which is the practice of denying loans or insurance to people based on their race or ethnicity.

- **Citibank:** As mentioned earlier, Citibank's predecessor, City Bank of New York, was founded by a slave trader and became one of the largest banks involved in financing the slave trade. Citibank has also been involved in other forms of discrimination, such as predatory lending and redlining.

- **Bank of America:** One of Bank of America's predecessors, Bank of Italy, was not directly involved in the slave trade, but it has been involved in other forms of discrimination, such as redlining and discriminatory lending practices.

- **The Bank of New York Mellon:** As mentioned earlier, The Bank of New York was founded by Alexander Hamilton, who was involved in the slave trade. The bank has also been involved in other forms of discrimination, such as predatory lending. Mellon Bank's predecessor, T. Mellon & Sons, was involved in financing the slave trade and owning slaves. Mellon Bank has also been involved in other forms of discrimination, such as redlining.

- **The National City Bank of New York** (now Citibank) was involved in financing the slave trade and owned slaves. The bank has also been involved in other forms of discrimination, such as redlining.

- **First National Bank of New York** (now Citibank) was involved in financing the slave trade and owned slaves. The bank has also been involved in other forms of discrimination, such as redlining.

- **Guaranty Trust Company of New York** (now JPMorgan Chase) was involved in financing the slave trade and owned slaves. The bank has also been involved in other forms of discrimination, such as redlining.

- **Chase National Bank** (now JPMorgan Chase) was involved in financing the slave trade and owned slaves. The bank has also been involved in other forms of discrimination, such as redlining.

- **Federal Reserve Bank of New York:** The Federal Reserve Bank of New York was not directly involved in the slave trade, but it was established to serve the interests of the larger banks, many of which were involved in the slave trade.

- **Brown Brothers Harriman (BBH)** played a crucial role in the establishment of the Federal Reserve System, the central banking system of the United States. In fact, the firm's senior partner, George Herbert Walker, was a member of the original group of bankers who met in secret on Jekyll Island in 1910 to draft the plan that would eventually become the Federal Reserve Act. As previously discussed, the bank's early success was built on the enormous profits generated from the transatlantic slave trade in its various forms.

While some of these banks no longer exist in their original form, their legacy of racism and discrimination continues to greatly influence the American financial system, culture and society at large. It is important to acknowledge and address these issues in order to create a more equitable and just society. These primary institutions of global capitalism must be held accountable for the inequality they created, profited from and continue to profit from.

It is important for both corporationns and governments to take accountability for their part in the slave industrial complex and

make just and fair compensation and restitution to slavery's victims for several reasons:

- **Justice:** Slavery was a grave injustice inflicted on millions of people over centuries, and its legacy of discrimination and inequality persists today. Holding those who benefited from and perpetuated this injustice accountable and making amends is a step towards righting past wrongs.

- **Repairing Harm:** Slavery caused significant harm to the individuals who were enslaved, their descendants, and their communities. Making restitution and reparations can repair some of the harm caused by slavery and its legacy, such as intergenerational poverty, lack of access to education and healthcare and ongoing discrimination.

- **Economic Justice:** Slavery was a major economic force that helped build the wealth of many corporations and governments. Making just compensation and restitution to slavery's victims in the same currency that was the purpose of their calamity represents economic justice in kind.

- **Reconciliation:** Acknowledging and taking responsibility for the role played in slavery by corporations and governments can help promote reconciliation between different groups and move towards a more just and equal society.

- **Moral Responsibility:** It is the moral responsibility of those who benefited from and perpetuated slavery (white people) to take accountability and make amends for their actions.

In conclusion, taking accountability for their part in the slave industrial complex and making just and fair compensation and restitution to slavery's victims is not only important for rectifying past wrongs and repairing harm, but also for promoting justice, reconciliation and a more equal society.

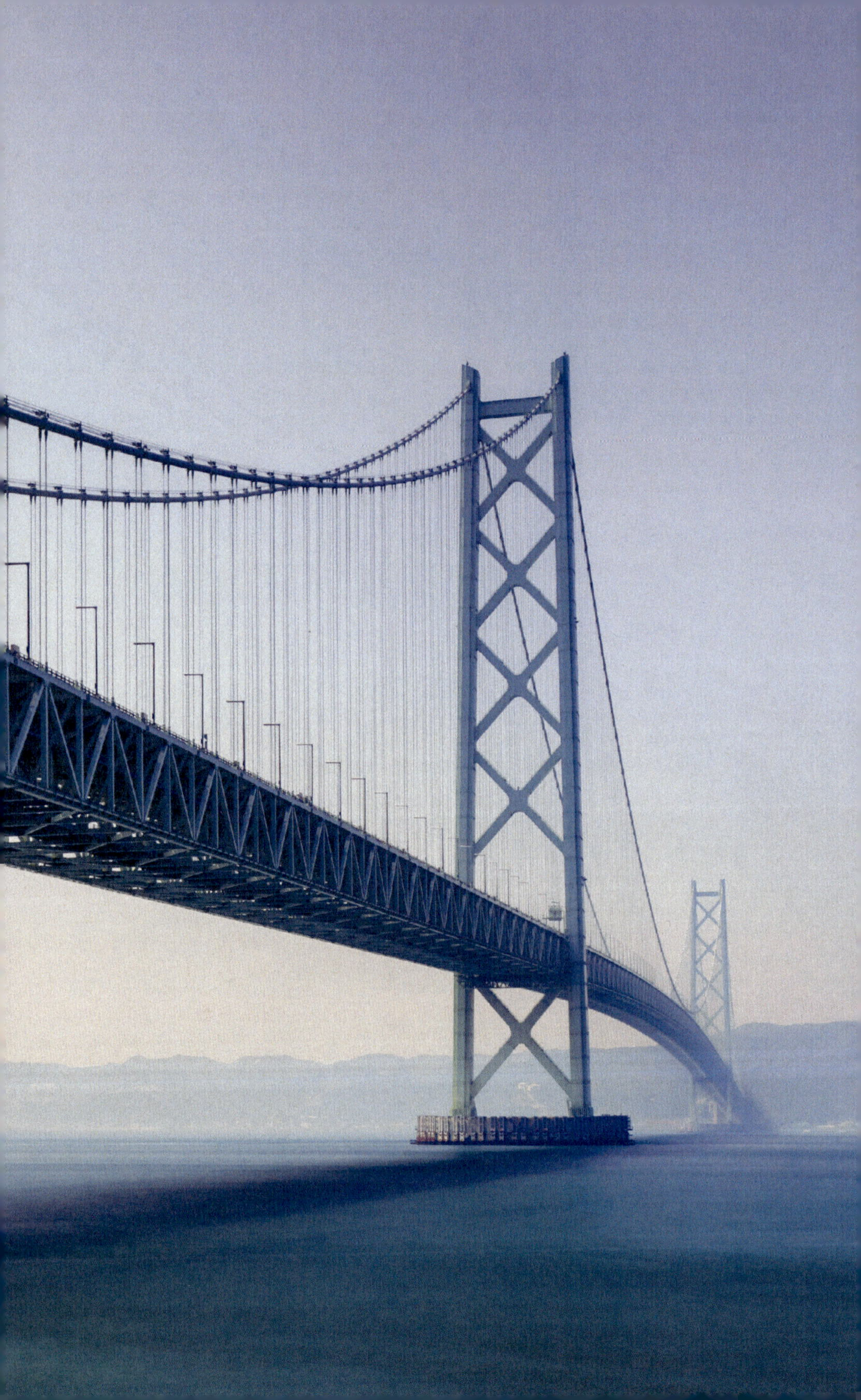

CHAPTER 5

MYTHS, MISCONCEPTIONS AND FOX NEWS

Reparations for slavery and its legacy is a controversial topic in the United States, with many myths and misconceptions surrounding the idea. In this chapter, we will expose, examine and debunk some of the common myths and misconceptions around reparations.

Misconception number one: Just how misleading the terms "slave" and "slave trade" actually are.

It should be said that in the year 2023 the terms "slave" and "slave trade" are toxic to the discussion and should be retired because they separate people from truly understanding the brutality and inhumanity of what chattel slavery actually was. The word "slave" in addition to being vague and remote, reduces people to their condition and history rather than acknowledging their humanity, agency and the fact that they were victims of a horrific system of oppression. This serves to further distance most of us from seeing ourselves or anyone we personally know in this light, and therefore creates a lack of connection or empathy for humans, just like them, trapped in a living nightmare that they cannot escape. The term "slave" reinforces a misconception that people of African descent were naturally and inherently inferior and destined for servitude. Similarly, "slave trade" is not only misleading but it is also a gross understatement of the true nature of the transatlantic slave industry. As mentioned earlier, the transatlantic slave trade was a complex system of human kidnapping, torture and trafficking, backed by governments and financed by wealthy individuals and institutions. It was a highly organized and profitable enterprise that lasted for over three centuries and was responsible for the forced migration of millions of Africans to the Americas. By reducing the slave industrial complex to an exchange of goods between simple traders, the term "slave trade" can downplay the systemic nature of slavery and the enormous profits that were generated from it. It can also perpetuate the false idea that slavery was a purely economic institution, rather than a deeply rooted social and political system of oppression that had lasting impacts on all enslaved Africans and their descendants.

The Myth that Reparations are Unnecessary Because Slavery Ended Long Ago and the Current Generation is not Responsible.

The fact is that the effects of slavery and discrimination have been passed down through generations of white and African Americans. The racial wealth gap, unequal access to education and healthcare, and over-representation in the criminal justice system are all rooted in a legacy of slavery and systemic racism. Reparations seek to address the generational harm caused by slavery and discrimination.

The Myth that Reparations will only Benefit a Small Group of African Americans who were Slaves or Directly Affected by Slavery

Reparations are not meant to be solely for those who were slaves, but for the entire community that has been impacted by centuries of slavery and discrimination. The generational wealth gap and systemic barriers have affected all 37 million African Americans, not just those who can trace their lineage back to enslaved individuals. The powers that be definitely know who Black Americans are when they want to sell something or target them for aggressive policing or other malfeasance.

The Myth that African Americans Should be Grateful for Progress and Stop Dwelling on the Past

Acknowledging the impact of slavery and discrimination is not dwelling on the past, but rather recognizing the reality of the present. It is important to acknowledge and address the ongoing harm caused by systemic racism in order to move forward as a society. Other detractors say that it would be unpatriotic to pay for the sins of the past. This myth ignores the fact that reparations are not just about acknowledging past injustices but also addressing their ongoing impact on the present.

Reparations are an investment in the future of America, as they have the potential to reduce inequality, increase economic growth and promote racial healing.

The Myth that Reparations Would be Too Expensive and Would Bankrupt the Country

The argument that reparations would be too expensive ignores the fact that the economic cost of slavery and its legacy has been immense. The wealth gap between Black and white Americans is estimated to be at least $10 trillion, and addressing this gap through reparations would be a long-term investment in the economic health of the country. Moreover, the cost of reparations could be offset by the economic benefits that would result from reducing inequality and increasing economic mobility. This is widely covered in the Who Pays? Section of chapter 4 of this book.

The Myth of Meritocracy

One of the most common arguments against reparations is the belief in meritocracy. The idea that America is a land of equal opportunity, where people are rewarded based solely on their hard work and talent, is deeply ingrained in the American psyche. However, this belief ignores the reality of systemic racism, and the role it has played in the economic and social advancement of white Americans.

For generations, African Americans were denied access to the same opportunities as their white counterparts. From slavery to Jim Crow laws and redlining, Black Americans have been systematically disadvantaged by policies and institutions that favored whites. As a result, the wealth gap between white and Black Americans is enormous, with the average white family having ten times the wealth of the average Black family. Anyone who would challenge this as fact must have their motives challenged and biases checked.

The myth of meritocracy is particularly insidious because it allows white Americans to absolve themselves of any responsibility for the economic disparities between the races. By insisting that America is a meritocracy, they can claim that any success they have achieved is solely due to their own hard work and talent, rather than the result of a system that privileges them and punishes African Americans and other non-whites.

The Myth That There Is No Systemic Racism in America

The claim that there is no systemic racism in the United States is often heard and controversial. While some individuals may argue that racism is a problem of the past or that it is limited to individual actions, the reality is that racism continues to be a pervasive problem in many aspects of American society.

Systemic racism refers to the ways in which racism is embedded in the policies, practices and norms of institutions and organizations, leading to disparities and inequalities that disproportionately affect a targeted group of individuals. Examples of systemic racism can be seen in housing, education, healthcare, the criminal justice system and other areas of American life. For example, eminent domain abuse and over-policing are just two examples of government systemic racism in the United States, which have been used as means for municipal revenue at the expense of minority communities.

Eminent domain abuse occurs when the government seizes private property for public use, often for the purpose of economic development or urban renewal, without just compensation or adequate consideration for the displaced residents. Minority communities are particularly vulnerable to eminent domain abuse, as they often lack the political and economic power to resist such actions. For example, Bruce's Beach was a Black-owned beach resort in Los Angeles that was seized by the city through eminent domain in 1924. The city, motivated by the desire to push out Black residents from the area, claimed that it needed the land to build a park. The city condemned the property and paid Willa and Charles Bruce $14,500. The land was never used for the park, and it remained vacant for decades until it was eventually sold to a private developer. After decades in court and several bitter defeats, their great grandchildren were awarded the property in 2022, now worth millions. The remains of dozens of once proud and thriving African American communities can be found under the many highways, civic auditoriums and arenas built around the country as they were often found to be cheap and suitable places to locate them by the city planners and developers of the times.

Over-policing refers to the disproportionate targeting and surveillance of minority communities by law enforcement, which leads to higher rates of arrests, convictions and incarceration. This not only perpetuates the cycle of poverty and disadvantage faced by these communities, but also generates billions in revenue for municipalities through fines, fees and forfeiture of property as well as lucrative government contracts for the housing, transportation, supervision and care of the incarcerated. For example, the Ferguson Police Department in Missouri was found to have engaged in unconstitutional and discriminatory practices against Black residents, including excessive force and illegal searches and seizures, backed by aggressive policies like "Stop and Frisk" in order to generate revenue for the city. The Department of Justice investigation into Ferguson's police practices following the death of Michael Brown brought national attention to the issue of over-policing and racial profiling. Studies have also shown that Black Americans are more likely to be stopped, searched and arrested by police compared to White Americans, even when controlling for factors like crime rates. They are also more likely to receive harsher sentences and face a higher risk of being wrongfully convicted. Similarly, Black and Hispanic Americans are more likely to live in neighborhoods with higher levels of poverty and environmental hazards. Research has consistently shown that people of color, particularly Black and Indigenous individuals, face significant disparities in access to quality healthcare, education, employment and housing, disproportionate levels of police brutality and incarceration, which are rooted in systemic racism.

In the workplace systemic racism is reflected in this African American proverb; "A Black person has to work twice as hard, to get half as far, for none of the credit." For Black people, this means that they often must work harder than their white counterparts to achieve the same level of success and recognition. They may face discrimination and bias in hiring and promotion decisions, as well as a lack of opportunities for advancement. Even when they do succeed, they may not receive the same level of credit or recognition as their white colleagues. In contrast, white mediocrity in the workplace refers to the phenomenon of white individuals being rewarded or promoted despite their lackluster performance or qualifications.

This can be attributed to white privilege, which refers to the societal advantages and benefits that white people receive because of their skin color, such as better job opportunities, access to education and healthcare, and more favorable treatment by the criminal justice system. This dynamic is evident in the persistent underrepresentation of Black individuals in leadership positions in many industries. Despite efforts to increase diversity and inclusion, the highest levels of management and leadership in many organizations remain overwhelmingly white. This lack of representation not only limits opportunities for Black individuals but also perpetuates a culture of white mediocrity, in which less qualified or less talented white individuals may be given preferential treatment over more qualified Black employees. These disparities and inequalities are not the result of individual actions or choices, but rather, the result of centuries long policies and practices that have perpetuated and passed down racism in American society, systemically.

In conclusion, the claim that there is no systemic racism in America is a dangerous myth that overlooks the pervasive nature of racism in American institutions and society. Systemic racism is obvious in disparities and inequalities that disproportionately affect people of color in areas such as housing, education, healthcare, the criminal justice system, and the workplace. This has resulted in a cycle of poverty and disadvantage for the Black American community. The issues of eminent domain abuse and over-policing are just two examples of government systemic racism that have been used to exploit African American communities for municipal revenue at their expense. Furthermore, the workplace is not immune to systemic racism, as Black individuals often must work twice as hard to achieve the same level of success and recognition as their white counterparts, while white mediocrity is generally promoted despite lackluster performance or qualifications. These disparities and inequalities are deeply rooted in American history and society, must be accounted for and dismantled through intentional policies and practices that promote diversity, equity, and inclusion.

The Myth of Critical Race Theory

The term "Critical Race Theory" (CRT) has been weaponized by those who oppose efforts to address systemic racism in America. CRT is an academic discipline that emerged in the 1970s and 1980s and seeks to examine the ways in which race and racism are intentionally embedded in America's financial, law and legal institutions. However, opponents of efforts to address systemic racism have mischaracterized CRT as a divisive ideology that seeks to "indoctrinate" students with a "hateful" and "divisive" worldview. This misrepresentation of CRT has been used as a rallying cry to oppose diversity, equity, and inclusion initiatives in schools and workplaces across the country. This is almost laughable as an argument as its premise is to in effect criminalize merely examining what is obviously based on data, apparent in the policy, practice, and operation of these institutions.

Conservative politicians and media outlets have used these terms to rally their base against any attempts to address systemic racism in America. They argue that discussions of race and racism are divisive, and that focusing on these issues only further divides the country. Avoiding discussions of race and ignoring the impact of historical and ongoing discrimination in reality, only perpetuates inequality and injustice. The conservative pushback against CRT can been seen in numerous ways, including through legislation aimed at banning the teaching of CRT in schools. For example, in June 2021, Florida's version of George Wallace, Governor Ron DeSantis signed a bill banning the teaching of CRT in K-12 schools in the state. The bill requires that "history be viewed as factual, not constructed," and prohibits teaching "that an individual, by virtue of his or her race or sex, is inherently racist, sexist, or oppressive." The bill has been widely criticized by those who argue that it is an attempt to whitewash history and stifle discussions of systemic racism in schools. It must be said that the facts are the facts, and the analysis is born out of the data that history produces, no matter what you call it. For example, the Rosewood massacre is a painful and tragic event in Florida's history, in which a predominantly Black community was destroyed by a white mob who murdered up to 100 innocent Black people in 1923. The event was covered up for decades, and only in recent years has the full extent of the horror been acknowledged. However, the passage of laws banning the teaching of Critical Race Theory (CRT) in schools, such as the one signed by Governor DeSantis, suggests that there are still significant obstacles to educating students about the history of racism and violence in America. The history of the slave industrial complex in America has not changed and the records are readily available should one do the research. Surely the state and its governor know this. Why would they not want their children to know what they obviously must know? Another example of how the term Critical Race Theory has been used to push back against progress is the recent controversy surrounding the implementation of anti-racism and

George Wallace wannabe, Rod DeSantis signs anti-truth legislation in Florida in 2021

diversity training programs in federal agencies and schools. In September 2020, former President Trump issued an executive order banning federal agencies from conducting any training that included concepts such as "white privilege" and "systemic racism," which he claimed were divisive and anti-American.

In addition to these legislative and executive efforts, the pushback against CRT has also taken the form of personal attacks on scholars and educators who advocate for CRT. Some have been subjected to harassment, threats, and even firings from their jobs. This has created a chilling effect on those who may want to engage in discussions about systemic racism or incorporate CRT into their teaching. The opposition to CRT and efforts to address systemic racism in America reveal the deep-seated resistance to change that exists in the country. It highlights the fact that acknowledging the existence of systemic racism requires acknowledging that the status quo benefits some groups while disadvantaging others. It also reveals that many Americans are uncomfortable with the idea that they may have benefited from systemic racism and may be resistant to efforts to rectify these inequalities. It is said that the toxic last resort of the intellectually defeated is backlash, and desperate displays of power including violence.

Similarly, the term "woke" has been used to disparage individuals or groups who advocate for social justice and equality, with the implication that they are overly sensitive or overly concerned with political correctness. It has become a way to dismiss conversations about privilege, systemic racism, and other issues related to equity and fairness. By framing these conversations in terms of catch-all phrases like "CRT" and "woke," opponents of social justice and equality can avoid grappling with the complexities of these issues and instead rely on simplistic, reductionist arguments that are often rooted in fear and defensiveness. The use of the term Critical Race Theory as a political wedge issue highlights the ongoing struggle for racial justice and equity in the United States and underscores the need for continued advocacy and activism on behalf of marginalized communities.

In conclusion, the opposition to CRT and efforts to address systemic racism in America are part of a broader resistance to change and a desire to maintain the status quo. The misrepresentation of CRT as a divisive ideology is a tactic used to discredit those who seek to address systemic racism and perpetuate the idea that America is a color-blind society. However, the reality is that toxic systemic racism continues to exist in America, and addressing it requires acknowledging its existence and taking steps to rectify the inequalities it creates.

The Myth That Reparations Would Create a Dependency Culture

Based on the racist assumption that Black Americans are inherently lazy or somehow unwilling to work hard. This assumption is not only racist but also ignores the systemic barriers that have prevented Black Americans from accessing the same opportunities as white Americans. Ironically, the opposite is the truth; NOBODY has worked and bled harder than African Americans in the soil of this country. Another irony is that one could easily call early America a dependent culture of free labor. Corporate America's bill for 246 years of unpaid wages to Black Americans alone lies in the trillions of dollars, and that's not ironic, it's a crime.

The Myth of Pseudo-Patriotism

Another common myth surrounding reparations is the idea that they are somehow un-American or unpatriotic. The argument is that by providing reparations, the government would be punishing innocent people for the sins of their ancestors, and that it goes against the principles of fairness and justice. However, this argument ignores the fact that the government has a long history of providing reparations to groups that have been wronged. For example, Japanese Americans who were interned during World War II were provided with reparations in 1988, and Native American tribes have received reparations for land taken from them by the government.

Some claim that the idea of patriotism is incompatible with the idea of reparations. In fact, reparations can be seen as a way to live up to the principles of America, such as equality and justice for all. By acknowledging the wrongs of the past and providing a remedy for them, America can move closer to the founding ideals it is so proud of.

The Role of Toxic Right-Wing Media and FOX News

Finally, right-wing media outlets such as Fox News have contributed to the dissemination of myths and misconceptions about reparations. These outlets often frame the issue in a way that pits African Americans against white Americans, perpetuating the idea that reparations would unfairly benefit one group at the expense of another. Additionally, they often use misleading statistics and rhetoric to downplay the effects of slavery and systemic racism on Black Americans, furthering the belief that reparations are unnecessary or even harmful. It is important to discuss the role of FOX News in shaping public opinion on reparations. FOX News has a well-documented history of promoting right-wing ideology and spreading misinformation on a range of issues, including reparations. In the case of reparations, FOX News and knock off outlets like Newsmax and OAN have consistently portrayed the idea as radical and divisive, using scare tactics to rally its conservative base against the idea. They have claimed that reparations would be unaffordable, unfair and would punish white Americans who had nothing to do with slavery. However, these arguments are not based in fact. Reparations, as we have discussed, are a legitimate way to address the economic and social disparities that were created by slavery and systemic racism. By perpetuating myths and misconceptions about reparations, FOX News is doing a disservice to its viewers and to the broader public discourse.

The traditional profit motive is probable cause for their approach to the subject as there are fortunes to be made in the hate-speech, culture-warmongering and disinformation business and nobody does it better (worse) than FOX News. In the case of FOX News, this involves the use of language and rhetoric that appear to be neutral or factual but are actually designed to reinforce negative stereotypes and biases towards African Americans. Another example of FOX News portrayal of African Americans as "welfare queens" or "lazy" by certain FOX News hosts and commentators. These terms are often used to imply that Black people are responsible for their own economic struggles and that they are not motivated to work hard or be successful. One of the most significant ways that FOX News promotes dog whistle racism is through its coverage of crime and criminal justice issues. The network frequently focuses on stories of violence and unrest in urban areas, portraying Black and brown people as criminals and "thugs" who are a threat to white, middle-class America. This coverage is often accompanied by images of burning buildings, angry protesters and police in riot gear, creating a sense of chaos and disorder that reinforces racial stereotypes and anxieties.

Critics argue that FOX News' dog whistle racism is not only morally wrong but also profitable, as it serves to attract and retain a large, dedicated audience that is willing to tune in for a daily dose of white superiority. Some have called for advertisers to boycott the network in response to its controversial coverage, while others have argued for regulatory action to hold the network accountable for its role in promoting and profiting from racial stereotypes and division.

Despite its controversial coverage, FOX News remains one of the most-watched cable news channels in the United States, with millions of viewers tuning in each day. The network's audience is largely white and conservative, and many experts believe that its coverage of race and racism plays a significant role in shaping the attitudes and beliefs of its viewers.

In summary, FOX News' and right-wing media's dog whistle racism is a significant problem in American media, playing an outsized role in shaping public attitudes and opinions about race and racism. As these networks continue to attract a large and dedicated audience, it is essential to hold them accountable for their role in perpetuating racial stereotypes and promoting division, and to work towards a more inclusive and equitable media landscape for all Americans.

To conclude, addressing and debunking these myths and misconceptions is essential to achieving the reconciliation and justice that the United States needs to move forward as a more equitable and just society. By acknowledging the harm that has been done and taking steps to redress it, we can work towards a future where all Americans can thrive and prosper regardless of their race or ethnicity.

THE PREVIOUS CHAPTERS HAVE ESTABLISHED:

1. The what, when, who, how, and why of the American slave industrial complex.

2. **The historic, ongoing consequences and effects of the slave** industrial complex on its oppressed victims and enriched perpetrators.

3. Proposed reparations as the only viable solution and support the solution with both historical examples of reparations payments and corporate perpetrators responsible who should pay the bulk of the restitution.

4. Present, discuss and respond to FAQ and all common objections...

And still there are a few "dummies" out there; holdouts who still have doubts or a "c'mon" attitude towards the information presented thus far.

The next chapter is for you...

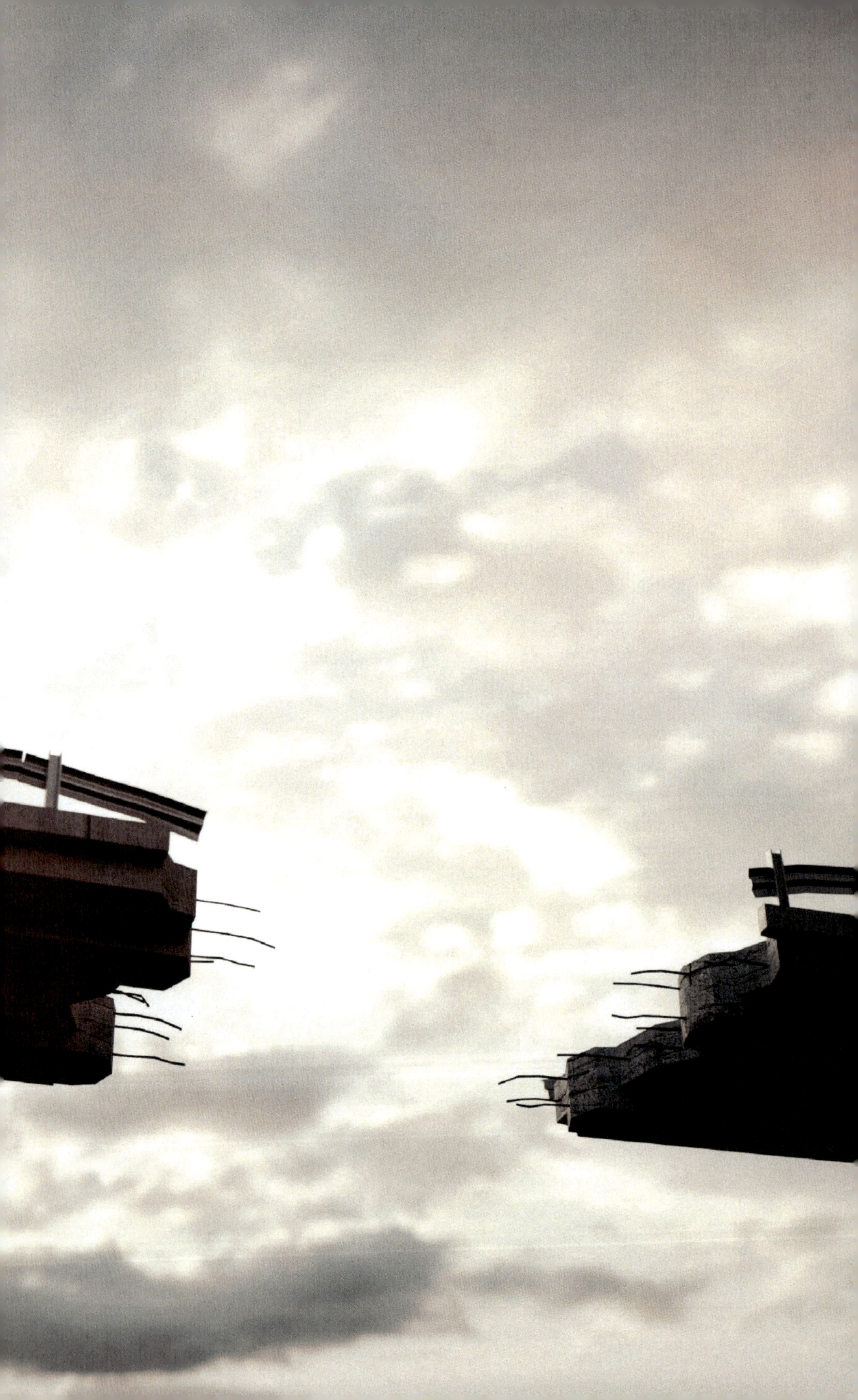

CHAPTER 6

THE RUB: MORALS, ETHICS, TOXIC WHITE GUILT AND COGNITIVE DISSONANCE IN A DIVIDED AMERICA

To the naked eye, the moral and ethical implications of reparations appear obvious. The United States was built on the enslavement and exploitation of African people, and the failure to provide reparations for that historical injustice is a continuing injustice in and of itself. Most people can agree that it is a moral obligation to rectify the wrongs of the past, and to ensure that the descendants of enslaved Africans are given the resources they need to build a better future for themselves and their communities. Furthermore, the idea of reparations is grounded in the principles of justice and fairness. Reparations seek to acknowledge the harms of the past, and to provide a measure of redress for those harms. From a moral and ethical perspective, this is the right thing to do. In addition, there is a practical argument for reparations.

Addressing the historic wealth and income inequalities between Black and white Americans through reparations would be a significant step towards creating a more equitable society. By providing resources to help build strong, thriving Black communities, the entire country would benefit from a healthier and more productive society. Reparations are not about punishment or blame, but about taking responsibility for the past and working towards a better future for all Americans. Informally, most Americans can objectively agree on all or almost all of this; however, we must now turn to the uncomfortable and complex issue of Toxic White Guilt syndrome.

Toxic white guilt is a complex and often misunderstood phenomenon that can have profound consequences for both individuals and society as a whole. One of the ways in which it manifests is through the creation of toxic white fear, which in turn can lead to toxic white brutality and overkill. The result is a vicious cycle that perpetuates itself and exacerbates existing racial tensions and inequalities. This cycle can be seen throughout American history, from the Nat Turner rebellion of 1831 to the deadly police encounters that continue to occur today. Nat Turner, a Black slave and reverend in Virginia, organized a rebellion against white slave owners that resulted in the deaths of over 50 white people. The rebellion was a response to the systemic oppression and violence that Turner and other slaves endured on a daily basis. However, the rebellion also led to a brutal and deadly response from white slave owners and their supporters, resulting in the deaths of hundreds of Black people. This toxic white overkill has its roots in the history of lynching in the United States, when white mobs would torture and kill Black people, often with the complicity of law enforcement and local authorities. This violence was used as a tool of terror to maintain white supremacy and control over Black communities. While lynching is no longer socially acceptable, the legacy of this violence lives on in the form of police brutality and other forms of state violence against Black people.

Dylan Roof killed 9 Black people in bible study at a church in Charleston, SC in 2015

The reaction to the rebellion was an example of how toxic white fear, which is the belief that marginalized communities pose a threat to white individuals and their power. This fear often results in excessive and violent responses towards these communities, as seen in the response to the Nat Turner Rebellion. Rather than addressing the root causes of the rebellion, white slave owners and their supporters responded with brutality and overkill, perpetuating the cycle of violence and oppression. One of the most infamous examples of toxic white overkill in recent history is the massacre perpetrated by Dylan Roof at the Emanuel African Methodist Episcopal Church in Charleston, South Carolina in 2015. Roof, a young white man with ties to white supremacist groups, walked into the church during a prayer service and opened fire, killing nine Black people. The idea of toxic white overkill can be traced back to the historical roots of white supremacy, slavery and racism in America. White people have long held a disproportionate amount of power and privilege in American society, and this has led to a deep sense of entitlement and superiority among some members of the white community. When faced with the prospect of losing some of their privilege or power, some white people may feel a sense of panic or anxiety that can lead to extreme behavior. This behavior can be seen in the mass shootings carried out by young white men, such as the Buffalo Tops Market massacre and the Charleston church shooting. In both cases, the shooters were motivated by a sense of racial hatred and a desire to assert their power over Black people.

The vicious cycle of toxic white guilt, fear, brutality and overkill continues to be perpetuated daily in modern society, particularly in deadly police encounters with Black people. The fear of Black people as a threat to white power has been ingrained in American culture for centuries, and it is reflected in the disproportionate use of force by police against Black individuals. In fact, it should be said that the history clearly shows Black people have always had more reasons to fear white

Retired cop Gregory McMichael murdered jogger Ahmaud Arbery in Georgia in 2022

people than white people have ever had to fear Black people...other than the moral and psychological weight of their collective inhumanity to a people who did them no harm. These encounters with police or even white neighborhood vigilantes often result in the deaths of innocent Black people, like Ahmaud Arbery a 25-year-old Black man, murdered in cold blood by Gregory McMichael, a retired police officer, and his son Travis McMichael, while jogging in a residential area in Georgia on February 23, 2020. It is important to recognize the role that toxic white guilt and fear play in perpetuating these systems of oppression. While acknowledging privilege and complicity in systemic oppression is necessary, it is important to address this guilt in a constructive and productive way, rather than allowing it to lead to negative consequences.

This means taking action to dismantle oppressive systems, rather than perpetuating them through fear and violence.

Toxic white guilt, fear, brutality and overkill syndrome is often accompanied by cognitive dissonance, a psychological term that describes the discomfort or mental stress experienced by a person who holds two or more contradictory beliefs, values or ideas. In the context of race and racism, cognitive dissonance can arise when a white person recognizes the injustice of their own privilege and the oppression of people of color, while also holding onto the belief in the superiority of whiteness or the myth of a color-blind society. This conflicting belief system can create anxiety and stress, leading to defensive or aggressive behavior. Similarly, in the case of deadly police encounters today, white police officers may feel threatened by Black people, especially in situations where there is a power imbalance. This fear can lead to excessive use of force, even when it is not warranted. This can result in the loss of innocent Black lives, as seen in the cases of Mike Brown, George Floyd, Breonna Taylor and so many others. To be clear, systemic racism and white supremacy have been ingrained in American society for centuries, and many white people have benefited from this system of oppression. This can lead to a reluctance to challenge or change the status quo, as it may require them to confront their own privilege and complicity in maintaining a system that oppresses others.

The persistence of this cycle can be attributed in part to a lack of accountability and acknowledgement. When white people are not held accountable for their actions, they are less likely to feel the psychological discomfort that cognitive dissonance creates. Furthermore, when the collective white consciousness denies or

Racially motivated massacre at Tops Supermarket in Buffalo, NY 2022

minimizes the existence of systemic racism, this only reinforces cognitive dissonance and the resulting cycle of toxic whiteness. Caucasians may be hesitant to admit that they benefit from white supremacy for several reasons. Firstly, admitting that one benefits from white supremacy would mean acknowledging that they have a societal advantage based on their race, which can be uncomfortable or even threatening to one's self-image and sense of fairness. It can be challenging to reconcile the idea that one has received advantages that others have not, particularly when these advantages have been taken for granted or not consciously recognized. White people may also be hesitant to admit that they benefit from white supremacy because of the potential consequences of such an admission. It could lead to criticism or backlash from others who do not want to acknowledge the existence of systemic racism or who may feel threatened by any suggestion of changing the status quo. Admitting the existence of white privilege may also lead to calls for reparations or affirmative action, which some white individuals may perceive as a threat to their own opportunities and success. Additionally, for those who have worked hard to achieve their own success, admitting that they have benefited from white privilege can feel like a personal attack on their achievements. The reluctance of white people to acknowledge their privilege and the benefits they receive from white supremacy highlights the deeply ingrained nature of systemic racism in American society. It also underscores the importance of ongoing education and efforts to raise awareness about the ways in which white privilege and white supremacy perpetuate inequality and harm to communities of color.

The topic of toxic white guilt syndrome is a complex and multifaceted phenomenon that represents a "dirty little secret" of Americana. While it may be difficult to overcome, recognizing and addressing this syndrome is a crucial step towards achieving a more just and equitable society. To that point, reparations are the only serious solution to break America's race disease and the cycle of toxic white guilt, fear, brutality and overkill, along with the cognitive dissonance that goes with it. The key to a healthier white American psyche lies in recognizing and addressing the root cause of this cycle, which is the legacy of brutal slavery and unjust systemic racism, even if they personally do not have anything against Black people, or never owned any slaves, or even if it happened a long time ago. To Black people, it never ended.

Toxic white guilt is rooted in the brutality and exploitation of their fellow human beings that white people have been responsible for. This burden of guilt manifests itself in a fear of retaliation or retribution from those they have harmed. This fear leads to a perceived need for control and the use of excessive force, which can result in brutality and overkill. When white people engage in acts of violence against Black people, they then experience internal conflict for their actions, leading to a cycle of toxic white guilt. This pattern is evident in the Nat Turner rebellion whose revolt against his white enslavers resulted in the deaths of at least 55 white people. In response, white mobs and militia forces went on a rampage, killing hundreds of Black people, many of whom were not involved in the rebellion. This overkill was a result of toxic white fear and the need for control, as well as a desire for retribution and revenge.

Today, we see this cycle of toxic white guilt, fear, brutality and overkill play out in deadly police encounters with Black people. Police officers who fear for their safety, whether justified or not, often resort to excessive force, resulting in the deaths of unarmed Black people. When this happens, the guilt and fear are compounded, and the cycle repeats. Reparations are the only real solution to break this cycle because they address the root cause of the problem. Reparations acknowledge the harm that has been done to Black people and offer a tangible way to make amends. **When white people take responsibility for the harm they have caused and actively work to make amends, the guilt and fear are diminished, and the cycle of violence is broken.**

Unarmed Mike Brown lies dead in the street as police look on in Ferguson Missouri in 2014

The lack of reparations also perpetuates the idea that the United States is a fundamentally unjust society. If the government cannot acknowledge and address the injustices of the past, it sends a message that it is not interested in creating a just society for all. This lack of justice and fairness is exactly what the population of white supremacists in America want. They want a society where white people are given preferential treatment, and where Black people are oppressed and kept in poverty. The United States' continued refusal to provide reparations to African Americans for the atrocities of slavery and segregation is not only a betrayal of justice and morality, but also provides aid and comfort to white supremacists who have long used the myth of white racial superiority to justify slavery and segregation. They have argued that Black people are inferior and do not deserve the same rights as white people. The denial of reparations to African Americans perpetuates this myth and sends a message that the government does not believe that Black lives matter. **This message is incredibly dangerous as it emboldens white supremacists and makes them feel validated in their racist beliefs.** Conversely, it greatly contributes to emotions of frustration and nihilistic hopelessness in Black people resulting in anger that can result in desperate acts of rage that we frequently see in the riots, looting and civil unrest that frequently accompany heinous acts of systemic brutality and overkill.

This disconnect between the United States' global image as a champion of freedom and justice and the country's history of denying justice and reparations to Black Americans has been a subject of much discussion and analysis. On one hand, the United States has presented itself as a beacon of democracy and human rights, promoting these values through its foreign policy and cultural exports. On the other hand, the country has a long history of racial injustice, including slavery, segregation, and ongoing systemic racism.

One key aspect of this disconnect is the United States' refusal to address the legacy of slavery and provide reparations to Black Americans. Reparations have been defined as compensation for past wrongs, and in the case of the United States, this would mean acknowledging the harms of slavery and providing compensation to descendants of enslaved people. Despite ongoing calls for reparations from Black Americans and other advocates, the United States has yet to take meaningful action on this issue.

Moreover, reparations are essential for creating a healthier white person in America. When white people acknowledge the harm, they have caused, and actively work to make amends, they can begin to heal the wounds that have been inflicted on their own psyches. By confronting the legacy of slavery and systemic racism, white people can begin to break free from the destructive cognitive dissonance that has enabled this cycle of violence to persist. Reparations have the best potential to promote healing and reconciliation between Black and white Americans. When white people take concrete actions to make amends for the past harm that they profited from and inflicted on Black people, it can begin to rebuild trust between the two groups. This, in turn, can create a more cohesive and united society, where all people are valued and respected. At the end of the day, isn't that worth a few bucks?

Reparations are the only real solution to break the cycle of toxic white guilt, fear, brutality and overkill that has plagued America for centuries. By acknowledging the harm that has been done to Black people and actively working to make amends, white people can begin to heal the wounds that have been inflicted on their collective psyches. Reparations have the potential to promote healing and reconciliation between Black and white Americans and create a more cohesive and unified society. It is time for America to take responsibility for its past and work for a better future for all.

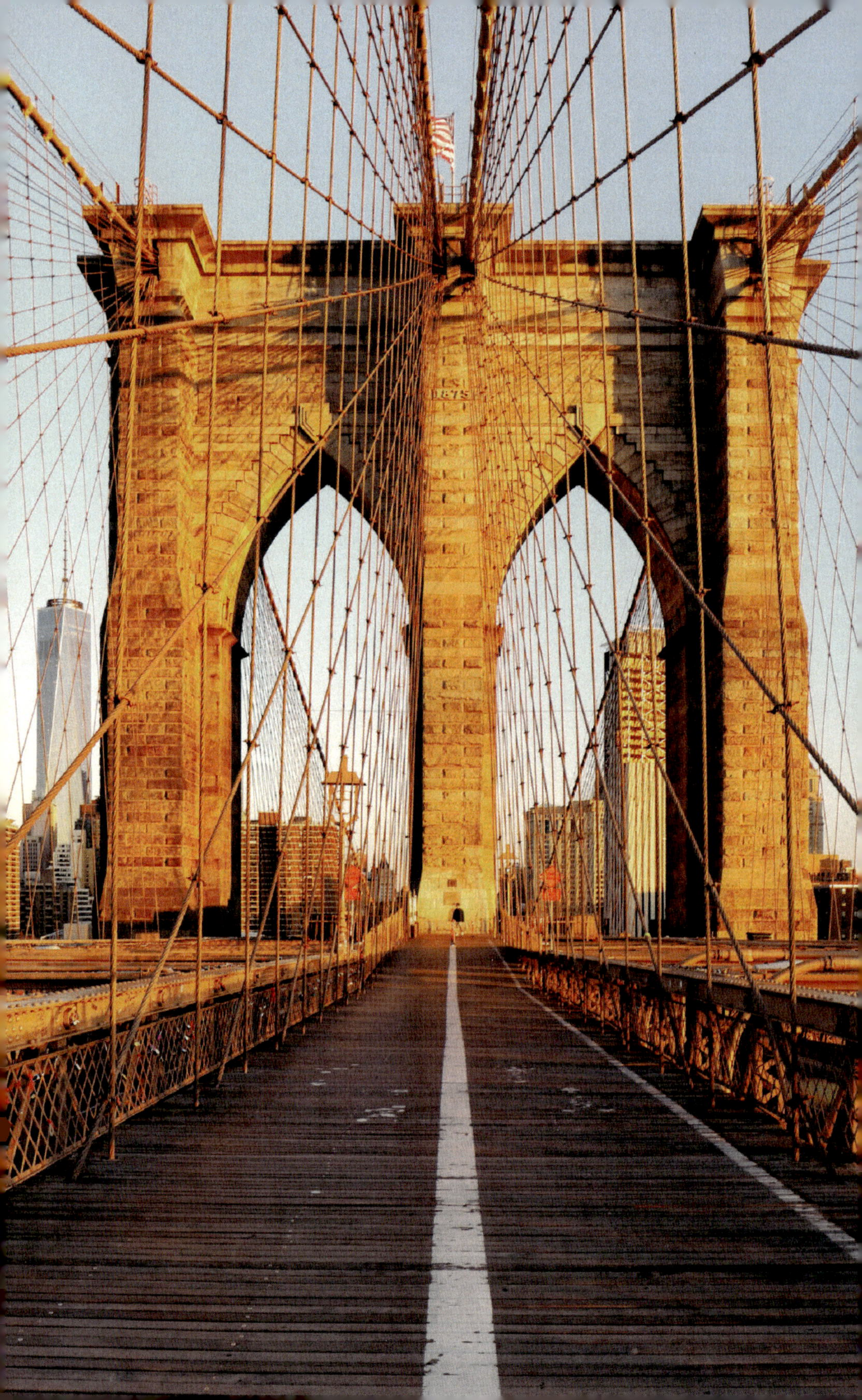
1875

CHAPTER 7

CONCLUSIONS

The undeniable truth is that the institution of chattel slavery was integral to the formation and success of the United States. The forced labor of kidnapped and enslaved Africans provided the foundation for the nation's economy, powering industries such as banking and finance, insurance, shipbuilding, agriculture, mining, railroads and textiles. Without the free labor of millions of enslaved people continually for 246 years it is indeed unlikely that the United States would have become the global superpower it is today. However, the exploitation and brutality that accompanied the institution of slavery cannot be ignored. Enslaved Africans were subjected to inhumane conditions, including beatings, rape and every form of physical, mental and economic violence that can be imagined, designed and constructed by the minds of men against his fellow man. The many traumas and lasting effects of this exploitation and brutality have been passed down through every generation of African Americans now for over 400 years. The legacy of the slave industrial complex continues to negatively impact African Americans today, evidenced in the American wealth gap where white households make ten times what a Black household earns... Ten times, and that's including Michael Jordan, Bob Johnson, Tyler Perry, Russell Simmons, Oprah, Will, Tiger, Ice Cube, Shaq, Dr. Dre, Jay-Z & Beyonce', and all the other Black millionaires in entertainment, the NBA and NFL combined. Is anyone seriously suggesting that white people are ten times smarter? Or work ten times harder than Black Americans? This enormous wealth chasm represents the "smoking gun" evidence in the case for reparations. Beyond any doubt, the practice and legacy of the slave industrial complex has created a structural disadvantage for Black Americans that cannot be overcome by simple individual "luck", hard work and merit alone. Most American grown-ups know this whether they acknowledge it or not.

In our hearts but rarely said, Americans know that systemic racism is a complex issue that has been difficult to address ultimately because, it benefits a section of the corporate capitalist superstructure, in the guise of white supremacy. White people (albeit some more than others) have historically and continue to benefit from the exploitation of people of color, and this has created a system that perpetuates inequality and disadvantage.

The status quo maintains power and control through the subjugation and exploitation of non-white individuals, and any attempts to dismantle it are met with fierce resistance from those who have and who continue to profit from it. This is undoubtedly the most challenging and uncomfortable aspect of this endeavor; to realize and acknowledge that there are "good people" in America who profit and benefit from the disenfranchisement, exploitation and oppression of others, particularly African Americans, and it must come to an end. To not say it here, is to render this entire volume inert.

The only serious remedy for this legacy is economic reparations. Reparations would provide a way to acknowledge the harm done and begin to repair the damage. It would at last be a concrete step towards addressing the systemic inequalities that continue to affect African Americans today. Reparations are not simply about giving money to individuals, rather they are about addressing the structural inequalities that have resulted from centuries of exploitation and oppression. This may also involve investments in education, healthcare and other areas that have been historically neglected in African American communities. Furthermore, reparations are not just a matter of justice, but also of morality and ethics. The United States has a responsibility to acknowledge and atone for the harm done to generations of African Americans by her hands. It is the right thing to do, and it is long overdue.

The denial of reparations to African Americans sends a message that their experiences of slavery, apartheid and systemic racism do not matter. It reinforces the notion that their suffering was insignificant, and that their ancestors' enslavement and exploitation were not serious crimes against humanity. This message is not only unjust, but it is also dangerous, as it feeds into the narrative of white supremacy, and fuels the anger and frustration that many African Americans feel towards the government and society as a whole.

When Black people see that the government and institutions continue to deny the impact of slavery and the systemic racism that followed, all rooted in the pursuit (love) of money, it further deepens the mistrust and alienation that many feel towards the system. It reinforces the narrative that the system was never intended to benefit Black people, and that their experiences of injustice and inequality are inevitable, ultimately because some more powerful and unseen entity profits from it. This sentiment often leads to frustration, anger and a sense of hopelessness, which can manifest in the form of protests, riots, civil unrest and suicidal/homicidal Black on Black crime.

Moreover, white supremacists view the denial of reparations as a validation of their beliefs. They use the historical denial of basic human rights to Black people as evidence of the supposed inferiority of Black people, and as justification for their belief in white racial superiority. This is dangerous because it feeds into their extremist beliefs and justifies their hatred and violence towards Black people. The entities that profit from oppression, division and carnage are the real winners. This is what cannot be ignored and must be addressed.

It is crucial for the government and institutions to recognize the impact of slavery and the ongoing effects of systemic racism. Providing reparations to African Americans is not only a moral obligation but a necessary step towards building a more just and equitable society. By acknowledging the past and working towards repairing the harm done, the government can demonstrate its commitment to racial justice, equity and equality. It is the only way to restore trust and confidence in the system and send a message that Black lives do after all, matter.

The impact of the slave trade on wealth and income inequality in America is transparently obvious. Slavery was the bedrock upon which the economic, political, education and social systems of the United States were built, and the legacy of this system is still largely intact today. In conclusion, the denial of reparations to African Americans is not just a moral failing; it is also a grievous political failure that undermines the very foundation of American democracy. It is long past time for the United States to acknowledge and address the legacy of slavery and segregation and disenfranchisement by providing reparations to those who have suffered from these atrocities. Reparations are a necessary step towards addressing the harm caused by the slave industrial complex and its most toxic side effect, systemic racism, and it is also essential to dismantle the structures of racism and white supremacy that continue to exist. Moreover, reparations for African Americans are necessary for the United States to truly achieve its higher self because they acknowledge past harms, address ongoing economic disparities, are a matter of justice and morality, and represent a critical step towards true reconciliation and healing between these two peoples at odds on this continent since the seventeenth century.

Finally, it must be said that being on the right side of history can be challenging and often requires courage, conviction and a willingness to stand up for what is right even in the face of adversity. It requires individuals to prioritize principles over personal gain and to work towards the greater good. Abraham Lincoln and Martin Luther King Jr. are examples of Americans who were on the right side of this history and fought for justice and equality for all at great personal cost. They prioritized the moral and ethical implications of their actions over personal gain and were willing to stand up against powerful institutions and social norms to promote change. Their legacies continue to inspire individuals to stand up for what is right and work towards a better world. Establishing reparations for African Americans in a serious and substantial amount and duration would not only fulfill the dreams and ideals of these heroes who were on the right side of history, but also finally begin the closing chapter in the American history book entitled "slavery and its aftermath."

The moral and ethical implications of being on the right side of history are significant. It can mean standing up against oppression, inequality and discrimination, and promoting fairness and justice for all individuals, even if it's inconvenient or uncomfortable. It can also mean working towards a more just and equitable society, even if it means challenging existing power structures and institutions. Only through this collective effort can we create a more just and equitable society for all who call themselves "American." All one needs to do is ask what side of history they are on. So, now I ask you, what side of history are you on?

Reparations 101 stands behind every word of the scholarship contained in this volume and looks forward to new and healthier discussions on this topic, and ultimately a healing that the races, this land and nation deserves. We invite you to share your thoughts and join the conversation at www.reparations-101.com

BIBLIOGRAPHY

CHAPTER 1

SECTION 1

- Berlin, I. (2003). Many thousands gone: The first two centuries of slavery in North America. Harvard University Press.
- Davis, D. B. (1966). The problem of slavery in Western culture. Cornell University Press.
- Eltis, D. (2017). The rise of African slavery in the Americas. Cambridge University Press.
- Klein, H. S. (1999). The Atlantic slave trade. Cambridge University Press.
- Mintz, S. W., & McNeil, S. (2016). The origins of African American cuisine. Routledge.
- Sobel, R. (2006). The Royal African Company. In The Encyclopedia of African-American Heritage (pp. 239-240). Infobase Publishing.
- Thomas, H. (1997). The slave trade: The story of the Atlantic slave trade, 1440-1870. Simon & Schuster.
- Williams, E. (1944). Capitalism and slavery. University of North Carolina Press.
- Barclays (2021). Slavery and Remembrance: 200 Years of Barclays. Retrieved from https://home.barclays/news/2021/07/slavery-and-remembrance--200-years-of-barclays.html
- Royal Bank of Scotland (2007). Royal Bank of Scotland Apologises for Historic Links to Slave Trade. Retrieved from https://www.rbs.com/rbs/news/2007/08/royal-bank-of-scotland-apologises-for-historic-links-to-slave-tr.html

- Craig Steven Wilder, Ebony and Ivy: Race, Slavery, and the Troubled History of America's Universities (New York: Bloomsbury Press, 2013).

- Ruth Simmons, "A Brief History of Slavery and the Origins of American Universities," The Journal of Blacks in Higher Education, no. 26 (Winter 1999-2000): 74-78.

- Leslie M. Harris, "Slavery and the University: Histories and Legacies," Slavery and Abolition, vol. 39, no. 2 (2018): 215-232.

- Eltis, David. "The volume and structure of the transatlantic slave trade: a reassessment." The William and Mary Quarterly 58, no. 1 (2001): 17-46.

- Klein, Herbert S. Slavery in the Americas: A Comparative Study of Cuba and Virginia. University of Chicago Press, 1986.

- Ortiz, Paul. Emancipation Betrayed: The Hidden History of Black Organizing and White Violence in Florida from Reconstruction to the Bloody Election of 1920. University of California Press, 2006.

SECTION 2

- Blackburn, R. (1997). The Making of New World Slavery: From the Baroque to the Modern, 1492-1800. Verso Books.

- Berlin, I. (1999). Generations of Captivity: A History of African-American Slaves. Harvard University Press.

- Davis, D. B. (1995). Inhuman Bondage: The Rise and Fall of Slavery in the New World. Oxford University Press.

- Johnson, W. (1999). The Chattel Principle: Internal Slave Trades in the Americas. Yale University Press.

- Rothman, A. S. (2000). Slave Country: American Expansion and the Origins of the Deep South. Harvard University Press.

- Simon, B. (2014). The New York Slave Revolt of 1712: A Prelude to the American Revolution. History Press.

- Rothbard, M. N. (1995). Conceived in Liberty. Ludwig von Mises Institute.

- Horton, J. O., & Horton, L. E. (2015). Slavery and the Making of America. Oxford University Press.

- Horton, J. O., & Blight, D. W. (2007). Slavery and Public History: The Tough Stuff of American Memory. The University of North Carolina Press.

- O'Toole, J. J. (2017). Robert Morris: Financier of the American Revolution. Simon and Schuster.

- Royal Bank of Scotland. (2018). RBS apologizes for its historical links to slavery. https://www.rbs.com/rbs/news/2018/04/rbs-apologises-for-its-historical-links-to-slavery.html

- Fernández, L. A. (2019). The slave trade in the archives of Lloyd's of London, 1760-1815. Routledge.

- Altman, D. (2020). Barclays apologizes for its history of slavery profiteering. The New York Times. https://www.nytimes.com/2020/07/23/business/barclays-slavery-profits.html

SECTION 3

- Berlin, Ira. Many Thousands Gone: The First Two Centuries of Slavery in North America. Harvard University Press, 1999.

- Foner, Eric. The Fiery Trial: Abraham Lincoln and American Slavery. W. W. Norton & Company, 2010.

- Genovese, Eugene D. Roll, Jordan, Roll: The World the Slaves Made. Vintage Books, 1976.

- Johnson, Walter. Soul by Soul: Life Inside the Antebellum Slave Market. Harvard University Press, 1999.

- Jones, Martha S. All Bound Up Together: The Woman Question in African American Public Culture, 1830-1900. University of North Carolina Press, 2007.

- McPherson, James M. Battle Cry of Freedom: The Civil War Era. Oxford University Press, 1988.

- Rothman, Joshua D. Notorious in the Neighborhood: Sex and Families Across the Color Line in Virginia, 1787-1861. University of North Carolina Press, 2003.
- Stampp, Kenneth M. The Peculiar Institution: Slavery in the Ante-Bellum South. Knopf Doubleday Publishing Group, 1956.
- White, Deborah Gray. Ar'n't I a Woman? Female Slaves in the Plantation South. W.W. Norton & Company, 1999.
- Alexander, M. (2012). The new Jim Crow: Mass incarceration in the age of colorblindness. The New Press.
- Collins, J. L. (2018). The Tulsa race massacre: A historical perspective. ABC-CLIO.
- Du Bois, W. E. B. (1935). Black Reconstruction in America: An Essay Toward a History of the Part Which Black Folk Played in the Attempt to Reconstruct Democracy in America, 1860–1880. Harcourt Brace.
- Gates, H. L. (2013). Life upon these shores: Looking at African American history, 1513-2008. Knopf.
- Lemann, N. (1991). The promised land: The great Black migration and how it changed America. Vintage Books.
- Painter, N. I. (2010). The history of white people. WW Norton & Company.
- Roberts, D. (2016). Killing the Black Body: Race, Reproduction, and the Meaning of Liberty. Vintage.
- Roediger, D. R. (2007). The wages of whiteness: Race and the making of the American working class. Verso.
- Sugrue, T. J. (1996). The origins of the urban crisis: Race and inequality in postwar Detroit. Princeton University Press.
- Terry, J. (2011). The New Plantation: Black Athletes, College Sports, and Predominantly White NCAA Institutions. Syracuse University Press.
- Washington, H. A. (2006). Medical apartheid: The dark history of medical experimentation on Black Americans from colonial times to the present. Anchor Books.

- Zinn, H. (2015). A people's history of the United States. Harper Perennial Modern Classics.

- Schwartz, M. A. (2005). The Nation's Capital and the White House. In A. J. A. Morris, The Columbia Guide to African American History Since 1939 (pp. 25-43). Columbia University Press.

- Slavery in the District of Columbia. (n.d.). Retrieved March 30, 2023, from https://www.nps.gov/articles/slavery-in-the-district-of-columbia.htm

- "The Yellow House: Vanished Washington D.C." by Lost Washington D.C. (https://lost-washingtondc.blogspot.com/2012/11/the-yellow-house.html)

- "The City and the Salve Trade" by Mary Beth Corrigan (https://www.washingtonpost.com/archive/lifestyle/magazine/2001/02/18/the-city-and-the-slave-trade/5f5dc5a6-c982-4b20-b930-547aa00c8cb6/)

- "District of Columbia Emancipation Act" by the National Archives (https://www.archives.gov/exhibits/featured-documents/dc-emancipation-act)

SECTION 4

- Foner, Eric. Reconstruction: America's Unfinished Revolution, 1863-1877. Harper Perennial, 2014.

- Blackmon, Douglas A. Slavery by Another Name: The Re-Enslavement of Black Americans from the Civil War to World War II. Anchor Books, 2009.

- Hine, Darlene Clark, et al. The African-American Odyssey: Combined Volume. Pearson, 2013.

- Rothstein, Richard. The Color of Law: A Forgotten History of How Our Government Segregated America. Liveright Publishing Corporation, 2017.

- Giddings, Paula J. Ida: A Sword Among Lions: Ida B. Wells and the Campaign Against Lynching. Harper Perennial, 2008.

- Goings, Kenneth W. The New African American Urban History. Routledge, 2018.
- Jones, James H. Bad Blood: The Tuskegee Syphilis Experiment. The Free Press, 1981.
- McGuire, Danielle L. At the Dark End of the Street: Black Women, Rape, and Resistance A New History of the Civil Rights Movement from Rosa Parks to the Rise of Black Power. Vintage Books, 2011.
- Garrow, David J. Bearing the Cross: Martin Luther King, Jr., and the Southern Christian Leadership Conference. Open Road Media, 2015.
- Alexander, Michelle. The New Jim Crow: Mass Incarceration in the Age of Colorblindness. The New Press, 2012.
- Forman Jr, James. Locking Up Our Own: Crime and Punishment in Black America. Farrar, Straus and Giroux, 2017.
- Roberts, Dorothy E. Killing the Black Body: Race, Reproduction, and the Meaning of Liberty. Vintage Books, 1998.
- Coates, Ta-Nehisi. Between the World and Me. Spiegel & Grau, 2015.

SECTION 5

- Alexander, M. (2012). The New Jim Crow: Mass Incarceration in the Age of Colorblindness. The New Press.
- Coates, T. N. (2014). The Case for Reparations. The Atlantic. https://www.theatlantic.com/magazine/archive/2014/06/the-case-for-reparations/361631/
- Eberhardt, J. L. (2019). Biased: Uncovering the Hidden Prejudice That Shapes What We See, Think, and Do. Viking.
- Kendi, I. X. (2019). How to Be an Antiracist. One World.
- Obama, B. (2020). A Promised Land. Crown.
- Rothstein, R. (2017). The Color of Law: A Forgotten History of How Our Government Segregated America. Liveright Publishing Corporation.

- Wilkinson, R. G., & Pickett, K. (2018). The Inner Level: How More Equal Societies Reduce Stress, Restore Sanity and Improve Everyone's Well-Being. Penguin Books.
- "George Wallace's Segregation Stand in Alabama School Door." History.com, A&E Television Networks, 27 Jan. 2010, www.history.com/this-day-in-history/george-wallaces-segregation-stand-in-alabama-school-door.
- Watkins, Mel. "George Wallace's 'Stand in the Schoolhouse Door' Is a Forgotten Prelude to Trump's Border Wall." The Guardian, Guardian News and Media, 11 Feb. 2019, www.theguardian.com/us-news/2019/feb/11/george-wallace-stand-in-the-schoolhouse-door-trump-border-wall.

CHAPTER 2

- Beckert, S. (2015). Empire of Cotton: A Global History. Vintage.
- Blackmon, D. A. (2008). Slavery by Another Name: The Re-Enslavement of Black Americans from the Civil War to World War II. Anchor.
- Davis, D. B. (2014). Inhuman Bondage: The Rise and Fall of Slavery in the New World. Oxford University Press.
- Guterl, M. P. (2001). The Color of Race in America, 1900-1940. Harvard University Press.
- Johnson, W. R. (1999). The Chattel Principle: Internal Slave Trades in the Americas. Yale University Press.
- Rothman, A. S. (1991). Slave Country: American Expansion and the Origins of the Deep South. Harvard University Press.
- Sven Beckert and Seth Rockman, "The Invention of American Capitalism," The American Historical Review 119, no. 1 (February 2014): 16–49.
- Walter Johnson, "On Agency," Journal of Social History 39, no. 4 (Summer 2006): 1135–1147.

- William Darity Jr. and A. Kirsten Mullen, From Here to Equality: Reparations for Black Americans in the Twenty-First Century (University of North Carolina Press, 2020).
- William Darity Jr., Darrick Hamilton, and Mark Paul, "A Roadmap to Reparations for African Americans," The American Prospect, September 17, 2018.
- Zinn, H. (2010). A People's History of the United States. Harper Perennial Modern Classics.

CHAPTER 3

- Anderson, C. (2020). JPMorgan Chase apologizes for ties to slavery, promises to do more. Reuters. https://www.reuters.com/article/us-jpmorgan-slavery/jpmorgan-chase-apologizes-for-ties-to-slavery-promises-to-do-more-idUSKCN24F2B9
- Bank of America. (2021). Our history. https://about.bankofamerica.com/en-us/our-story/our-history.html
- Brown University. (2021). Slavery and justice: Report of the Brown University Steering Committee on Slavery and Justice. https://www.brown.edu/about/administration/institutional-diversity/slavery-and-justice
- Deutsche Bank. (2019). Deutsche Bank apologizes for its role in the Holocaust. Deutsche Bank Newsroom. https://www.db.com/newsroom_news/2019/deutsche-bank-apologizes-for-its-role-in-the-holocaust-en-11491.htm
- Human Rights Watch. (n.d.). What are reparations? https://www.hrw.org/legacy/advocacy/race/reparations.htm
- New York Life. (2021). Our history. https://www.newyorklife.com/about/our-history
- United Nations. (2005). Basic principles and guidelines on the right to a remedy and reparation for victims of gross violations of international human rights law and serious violations of international humanitarian law. https://www.ohchr.org/en/professionalinterest/pages/remedyandreparation.aspx

- Volkswagen Group. (2021). Volkswagen Group history. https://www.volkswagenag.com/en/group/history.html

- Wachovia. (n.d.). Slavery and justice. http://www.wachovia.com/vision/slavery.jsp

- Wehner, T. (2020). Germany pays billions to Holocaust survivors. Deutsche Welle. https://www.dw.com/en/germany-pays-billions-to-holocaust-survivors/a-53547091

- Brown-Nagin, Tomiko. "Universities and Slavery: Bound by History." The Harvard Crimson, 2016, https://www.thecrimson.com/article/2016/3/3/universities-and-slavery-bound-by-history/.

- Craig Steven Wilder. Ebony and Ivy: Race, Slavery, and the Troubled History of America's Universities. New York: Bloomsbury Press, 2013.

- Duster, Alfreda M., et al. "Slavery and the Making of America's Elite Colleges and Universities." The Journal of Blacks in Higher Education, no. 58, 2007, pp. 96–101. JSTOR, https://www.jstor.org/stable/25073421.

- Hsu, Charlotte. "Harvard Owned Slaves, Professors Research Finds." The Harvard Crimson, 2011, https://www.thecrimson.com/article/2011/2/21/harvard-slavery-faculty-research/.

- Jones, Martha S. "Slavery and the University of Virginia." Encyclopedia Virginia, 2013, https://www.encyclopediavirginia.org/slavery_and_the_university_of_virginia.

- McMurtrie, Beth. "Georgetown's Slavery Legacy." The Chronicle of Higher Education, 2016, https://www.chronicle.com/article/georgetowns-slavery-legacy/.

- Ruderman, Wendy. "Yale, Slavery and Abolition." Yale Alumni Magazine, 2016, https://yalealumnimagazine.com/articles/4338-yale-slavery-and-abolition.

- Salam, Maya. "Brown University Grapples With Its Ties to Slavery." The New York Times, 2016, https://www.nytimes.com/2016/10/06/us/brown-university-slavery.html.

- Strauss, Valerie. "Universities Confront Their Links to Slavery." The Washington Post, 2016, https://www.washingtonpost.com/news/grade-point/wp/2016/03/28/universities-confront-their-links-to-slavery/.

- Wilder, Craig Steven. "The Racialized History of Higher Education in America." The Atlantic, 2016, https://www.theatlantic.com/education/archive/2016/11/the-racialized-history-of-higher-education-in-america/507856/.

CHAPTER 4

- Coates, Ta-Nehisi. "The Case for Reparations." The Atlantic, May 2014.

- Baptist, Edward E. The Half Has Never Been Told: Slavery and the Making of American Capitalism. Basic Books, 2014.

- Rothstein, Richard. The Color of Law: A Forgotten History of How Our Government Segregated America. Liveright Publishing Corporation, 2017.

- United Nations. "Report of the Working Group of Experts on People of African Descent on its mission to the United States of America." United Nations Human Rights Council, August 2016.

- Adamson, T. (2020, August 21). 13 Fortune 500 Companies That Benefited From Slavery. Forbes. Retrieved from https://www.forbes.com/sites/tommybeer/2020/08/21/13-fortune-500-companies-that-benefited-from-slavery/?sh=8e91f217d01b

- Coates, T. N. (2014). The case for reparations. The Atlantic. Retrieved from https://www.theatlantic.com/magazine/archive/2014/06/the-case-for-reparations/361631/

- Haygood, W. (2016). The Butler: A Witness to History. Atria Books.

- Massie, R. K. (2018). Slavery and the American West: The Eclipse of Manifest Destiny and the Coming of the Civil War. University of North Carolina Press.

- Roy, A. (2020, July 30). America's corporate giants must acknowledge their ugly histories of slavery. The Guardian. Retrieved from https://www.theguardian.com/commentisfree/2020/jul/30/americas-corporate-giants-must-acknowledge-their-ugly-histories-of-slavery

CHAPTER 5

- Coates, Ta-Nehisi. "The Case for Reparations." The Atlantic, June 2014. https://www.theatlantic.com/magazine/archive/2014/06/the-case-for-reparations/361631/

- Kendi, Ibram X. How to Be an Antiracist. One World, 2019.

- Rothstein, Richard. The Color of Law: A Forgotten History of How Our Government Segregated erica. Liveright Publishing Corporation, 2017.

- Taylor, Keeanga-Yamahtta. From #BlackLivesMatter to Black Liberation. Haymarket Books, 2016.

- Theoharis, Jeanne, and Brian Purnell. "Reparations and the Movement for Black Lives: A Response to the Democratic Presidential Candidates." The Nation, February 2020. https://www.thenation.com/article/politics/reparations-Black-lives-matter/

- Williams, Heather Andrea. Self-Taught: African American Education in Slavery and Freedom. University of North Carolina Press, 2005.

- Zinn, Howard. A People's History of the United States. Harper & Row, 1980.

- The New York Times. (2020, September 22). Trump Bars Federal Agencies From Some Racial Sensitivity Training. https://www.nytimes.com/2020/09/22/us/politics/ trump-race-sensitivity-training.html

- The Washington Post. (2021, April 8). The Republican campaign against Critical Race Theory may be backfiring. https://www.washingtonpost.com/politics/2021/04/08/republican-campaign-against-critical-race-theory-may-be-backfiring/

- NBC News. (2021, May 10). Critical race theory, explained. https://www.nbcnews.com/news/nbcblk/critical-race-theory-explained-n1266179

- Delgado, R., & Stefancic, J. (2017). Critical race theory: An introduction. NYU Press.

- DiAngelo, R. (2018). White fragility: Why it's so hard for white people to talk about racism. Beacon Press.

- Powell, J. A. (2021). The legal construction of race. In S. L. Kagan & L. D. Smith (Eds.), Race and the law (pp. 13-25). West Academic Publishing.

- Almonte, R. (2021). The battle over critical race theory and what it means for the classroom. PBS NewsHour. Retrieved from https://www.pbs.org/newshour/education/the-battle-over-critical-race-theory-and-what-it-means-for-the-classroom

- Rothstein, R. (2017). The case for reparations. The Atlantic. Retrieved from https://www.theatlantic.com/magazine/archive/2014/06/the-case-for-reparations/361631/

- Tate, C. (2021). Florida's new ban on critical race theory is an attempt to rewrite history. The Conversation. Retrieved from https://theconversation.com/floridas-new-banon-critical-race-theory-is-an-attempt-to-rewrite-history-162150

- The Leadership Conference on Civil and Human Rights. (2021). Reparations. Retrieved from https://civilrights.org/policy/reparations/

CHAPTER 6

- Coates, Ta-Nehisi. "The Case for Reparations." The Atlantic, June 2014, https://www. theatlantic.com/magazine/archive/2014/06/the-case-for-reparations/361631/

- Davis, Angela Y. "Are We Ready to Talk About the Role of White Supremacy in Perpetuating Toxic Whiteness?" The Nation, September 2017, https://www.thenation.com/article/archive/are-we-ready-to-talk-about-the-role-of-white-supremacy-in-perpetuating-toxic-whiteness/

- DiAngelo, Robin. White Fragility: Why It's So Hard for White People to Talk About Racism. Beacon Press, 2018.

- Kendi, Ibram X. How to Be an Antiracist. One World, 2019.

- Kivel, Paul. Uprooting Racism: How White People Can Work for Racial Justice. New Society Publishers, 2017.

- Steele, Shelby. "The Age of White Guilt." The Wall Street Journal, January 2006, https://www.wsj.com/articles/SB113834531652364707

- Tatum, Beverly Daniel. "Why Are All the Black Kids Sitting Together in the Cafeteria?": And Other Conversations About Race. Basic Books, 1997.

- "Charleston church shooting." Southern Poverty Law Center. https://www.splcenter.org/hatewatch/2015/06/17/charleston-church-shooting

- "White nationalist hate groups." Anti-Defamation League. https://www.adl.org/education/resources/backgrounders/white-nationalist-hate-groups

- "The legacy of lynching." Equal Justice Initiative. https://eji.org/news/lynching-in-america/

- "Hate crimes in America." FBI. https://www.fbi.gov/investigate/civil-rights/hate-crimes

CHAPTER 7

- Coates, T. (2014). The case for reparations. The Atlantic. Retrieved from https://www. theatlantic.com/magazine/archive/2014/06/the-case-for-reparations/361631/

- Darity Jr, W. A., & Mullen, A. K. (2019). From Here to Equality: Reparations for Black Americans in the Twenty-First Century. The University of North Carolina Press.

- Marable, M. (2011). The Myth of Post-Racial America. Monthly Review Press.

- Martin, M. (2021). Redlining and Homeownership in 20th Century America. Center for American Progress. Retrieved from https://www.americanprogress.org/issues/race/ reports/2021/04/12/497911/redlining-homeownership-20th-century-america/

- Rothstein, R. (2017). The Color of Law: A Forgotten History of How Our Government Segregated America. Liveright Publishing.

- Saito, N. (2021). The Case for Reparations in America. Cambridge University Press.

- Alexander, Michelle. The New Jim Crow: Mass Incarceration in the Age of Colorblindness. The New Press, 2012.

- Coates, Ta-Nehisi. Between the World and Me. Spiegel & Grau, 2015.

- Davis, Angela Y. Women, Race, & Class. Vintage Books, 1983.

- Anderson, E. (2015). The White Space. The Atlantic. https://www.theatlantic.com/magazine/archive/2015/09/the-white-space/399237/

- Bonilla-Silva, E. (2017). Rac

Made in the USA
Middletown, DE
14 October 2024